THE ADMINISTRATIVE
PRESIDENCY

THE ADMINISTRATIVE PRESIDENCY

Richard P. Nathan
Princeton University

JOHN WILEY & SONS
New York   Chichester   Brisbane   Toronto   Singapore

Library of Congress Cataloging in Publication Data:

Nathan, Richard P.
The administrative presidency.

Includes index.
1. Executive power—United States. 2. Administrative agencies
—United States—Management. 3. Nixon, Richard Milhous,
1913—   . 4. Reagan, Ronald. 5. United States—Politics and
government—1969–1974. 6. United States—Politics and
government—1981–
I. Title.

JK518.N389   1983   353.03'2   82-23712
ISBN 0-471-86871-X

Printed in the United States of America

10 9 8 7 6 5 4 3 2 1

For Mary

PREFACE

This book updates one written eight years ago on the administrative strategy for domestic affairs that Richard Nixon developed for his second term but which was aborted as a consequence of Watergate.* The essential question raised in the original book was whether and how the president of the United States should manage the federal bureaucracy. This new volume is different from the earlier book in two respects. It takes a much stronger position, arguing that elected chief executives—presidents, governors, mayors—and their appointees should play a larger role in administrative processes. It also contains an analysis of the experience of the Reagan administration, which in its first two years in office has demonstrated acumen and success in pursuing its major domestic policy goals through administrative actions. In the spirit of truth in advertising, I should make clear that I have considerable personal reservations about the domestic policies of the Reagan administration. Nevertheless, I have come to the conclusion that the basic approach to administration adopted by Ronald Reagan is the right one for the American presidency in the current period.

The focus of this book is on the role of the president as a manager. The examination here of the Nixon and Reagan experiences brings to life vital issues of contemporary governance that tend to be treated in a mechanical and uninteresting way in the literature of public administration.

I am indebted to a number of people who have encouraged me to extend my work in this area and have helped me to do so. My colleague Fred I. Greenstein at Princeton has been especially helpful and has been a patient and perceptive reader. A number of busy officials of the Reagan administration have been generous with their time in granting me interviews. Mark Mochary of John Wiley & Sons urged me to undertake this revision and was understanding when, in the usual way, it turned out to take considerably longer than I had originally planned. A number of people provided research assistance, particu-

---

*The title of the earlier volume was *The Plot that Failed: Nixon and the Administrative Presidency* (New York: John Wiley & Sons, 1975).

larly Rita Seymour and Lawrence Hamdan. David Aiken edited the manuscript, and Michele Pollak typed it.

The first book I wrote on this subject was dedicated to my wife, Mary M. Nathan, and so is this sequel. Her suggestions have found their way into the text in many places. But, in the usual manner, while I am grateful to a number of people who helped me, all of the ideas and descriptions presented in this book are ultimately and fully my responsibility.

RICHARD P. NATHAN

CONTENTS

INDEX

CHAPTER 1

The Administrative Presidency Revisited

This book is about one dimension of the presidency—the president's role as a manager in domestic affairs. It deals with the relationship between bureaucrats and politicians, which is a central issue of public administration. The term "bureaucrat" refers to career officials, many of whom have tenure rights as part of a civil service system. The term "politician" refers to elected officials, whose term in office is limited, and the men and women they appoint to assist them. Political officials include the loftiest politician of them all, the president of the United States. But the central question of the book is just as important for governors, mayors, county executives, and their appointees as it is for the presidency: *To what extent and in what ways should politicians manage the bureaucracy?*

The book has two purposes: (1) to argue that it is appropriate—in fact, desirable—for political chief executives to seek to exert greater managerial influence over the bureaucracy; and (2) to show how this has been an objective of two presidents, Richard Nixon and Ronald Reagan. Though both are conservative (Reagan much more so than Nixon), an administrative presidency strategy is appropriate and desirable for both liberals and conservatives.

A CHALLENGE TO PRESIDENTS

When he was president, John F. Kennedy reportedly once told a caller, "I agree with you, but I don't know if the government will." Whether Kennedy actually said this or not, the remark dramatizes an issue that has been less explored than other aspects of the presidency—the president's relationship to the bureaucracy. Harry Truman is reported to have complained, "I thought I was the president, but when it comes to these bureaucrats, I can't do a damn thing."[1]

Presidential scholar Clinton Rossiter speculated that many presidents would have considered this their hardest job, "not to persuade Congress to support a policy dear to his political heart, but to persuade the pertinent bureau or agency—even when headed by men of his own choosing—to follow his direction faithfully and transform the shadow of the policy into the substance of the program."[2]

Jimmy Carter's experience, perhaps more than others among recent presidents, illustrates the wisdom of Rossiter's remark. In a press conference in 1980, the final year of his presidency, Carter said, "Before I became president, I realized and was warned that dealing with the federal bureaucracy would be one of the worst problems I would have to face. *It has been worse than I had anticipated.*"[3]

The U.S. Constitution hedges on the role of the president as a manager. Article II, section 1 vests executive power in a president. Yet other provisions assign powers to Congress in ways that water down this assignment. Congress, for example, is empowered to create positions that can be "vested in the heads of department." It has used this power to assign statutory authority to specific officials at or below cabinet rank, instead of to the president. Other powers of the Congress—for instance, those to appropriate funds, conduct investigations, and override vetoes, and that of the Senate to confirm presidential appointees—have also over the years blurred the executive power assigned to the president in Article II.

In his classic study of the presidency, Edward S. Corwin referred to the words "executive power" in Article II as a "term of uncertain content."[4] Each president, he said, gives it his own expression. A president's relationship to the bureaucracy does not depend so much on the law, but on his own strategy, constituencies, and constitutional premises. Presidents have tried different strategies to exert their executive authority.

[1]As quoted in Burt Schorr and Andy Pasztor, "Reaganites Make Sure That the Bureaucracy Toes the Line on Policy," *Wall Street Journal*, February 10, 1982, p. 1.

[2]Clinton Rossiter, *The American Presidency* (New York: New American Library, 1956), p. 42.

[3]As quoted by Haynes Johnson, "Test," *The Washington Post*, April 30, 1978, p. 3. Italics added.

[4]Edward W. Corwin, *The President: Office and Powers* (New York: New York University Press, 1957), p. 3.

THREE CORE VALUES OF AMERICAN PUBLIC ADMINISTRATION

Political scientist Herbert Kaufman has identified three core values of American public administration that have been pursued at different periods of our history. The first, *representativeness*, dates from colonial times and reflects the mistrust of the king and royal governors that was expressed in the denunciation "taxation without representation." It resulted, particularly at the state level, in what Kaufman calls "the enthronement of the legislature."[5] The chief executive was viewed warily, both in his legislative and administrative role. The second period of American public administration for Kaufman is characterized by the value of *neutral competence*. It began in the mid-nineteenth century as a reaction to corruption in government, and is reflected in the civil service movement, which emphasized professionalism and merit. The third period of American public administration is characterized by what Kaufman calls *"the quest for executive leadership."* It began in the early twentieth century and is reflected in the development of executive budget systems and the strengthening of the office of the presidency under Franklin D. Roosevelt.[6] It is this period that is of greatest interest for our consideration of the role of the president in managing the bureaucracy.[7]

MODERN THEORIES OF PRESIDENTIAL MANAGEMENT

In 1936, President Roosevelt appointed a Committee on Administrative Management, headed by management expert Louis Brownlow. The Brownlow committee submitted its report ten months later. The report emphasized the necessity for a strong executive in a democracy, which it said was the unique contribution of the Founding Fathers. It urged changes to carry out this historic design. At points, the Brownlow report became so eloquent on this theme that it was almost embarrassing.

> A weak administration can neither advance nor retreat successfully—it can merely muddle. Those who waiver at the sight of needed power are false friends of modern democracy. Strong executive leadership is essential to democratic government today. Our choice is not between power and no power, but between responsible but capable popular government and irresponsible autocracy.[8]

---

[5]Herbert Kaufman, "Emerging Conflicts in the Doctrines of Public Administration," *American Political Science Review*, vol. 50, no. 4, December 1956, p. 1059.

[6]*Ibid.*, p. 1062.

[7]The terms "administration" and "management" are used interchangeably in this book to refer to the implementation or execution of policy.

[8]*Report of the President's Committee on Administrative Management*, January 1937, p. 53.

The Brownlow committee called for a basic regrouping of executive agencies. "Just as the hand can cover but a few keys on the piano, so there is for management a limited span of control."[9] The Brownlow committee called for the establishment of "12 great departments directly responsible in administration to the chief executive."[10]

The Brownlow report, however, is not as interesting as what FDR said about it. In submitting the report to Congress and also endorsing all of its recommendations, Roosevelt said:

> The plain fact is that the present organization and equipment of the executive branch of the Government defeats the constitutional intent that there be a single responsible Chief Executive to coordinate and manage the departments and activities in accordance with the laws enacted by the Congress. Under these conditions the Government cannot be thoroughly effective in working, under popular control, for the common good.[11]

Some of Roosevelt's proposals that were implemented (notably the creation of the Executive Office of the President) have given the modern presidency management tools used with different degrees of interest and skill since then. But they have not cooled the ardor of those who have followed in this tradition and urged that the president's role as chief executive be further strengthened.

The Brownlow committee's views on presidential management were again expressed in the postwar period in the work of the first Commission on the Organization of the Executive Branch of Government, under former President Herbert Hoover. This commission was appointed by President Harry S. Truman in 1947 and issued its report in March 1949. Its work reflects the same classical management view as that of the more outspoken Brownlow committee a decade earlier. It stressed accountability. The commission called for a "clear line of command from top to bottom." Like the Brownlow committee, the Hoover commission recommended expanding the president's staff and regrouping federal programs according to major functions under the direction of a small group of agency heads who they said should be regarded as "the president's principal assistants."

Besides the Brownlow and Hoover reports, there have been management councils under almost every president since FDR. In characteristic fashion, President Lyndon B. Johnson's council on organization and management operated in secrecy. Its report pulled no punches in diagnosing the problem. The federal government, it said, "is badly organized."

[9]*Ibid.*, p. 34.
[10]*Ibid.*
[11]*Ibid.*, p. iv.

Top political executives—the President and Cabinet Secretaries—preside over agencies which they never own and only rarely command. Their managerial authority is constantly challenged by powerful legislative committees, well-organized interest groups, entrenched bureau chiefs with narrow program mandates, and the career civil service.[12]

The Johnson task force, chaired by railroad executive Ben W. Heineman, was critical of domestic programs. Its conclusion in this area is of particular interest.

Many domestic social programs are under severe attack. *Some criticism is political.* It comes from those who oppose the goals of these national programs. *Some criticism stems from deflated hopes*, with current funding levels well below ultimate need and demand. *Some criticism arises because of alleged organizational and managerial weaknesses.* After several months of study, we believe the organizational criticism is merited.[13]

The Heineman task force also called for stronger institutional machinery for policymaking and coordination in the White House and urged measures to strengthen agency management structures and reduce the number of domestic agencies.

The steady progression of reports calling for measures to strengthen the management control of the presidency was broken as a result of the Watergate scandal. In a report prepared in 1974 for the special Senate investigative committee headed by Senator Sam J. Ervin, Jr., the National Academy of Public Administration rejected plans that Nixon had developed for his second term to centralize executive management. The authors, breaking sharply with tradition, emphasized, "the necessarily pluralistic nature of the federal establishment."[14] Although in many ways the descendants of the authors of the Brownlow and Hoover commissions, the National Academy panel breathed a sigh of relief that Watergate had prevented Nixon from implementing his elaborate plans.

Sandwiched between Nixon and Reagan were Presidents Gerald R. Ford and Jimmy Carter. Neither was strong in terms of exercising control over the bureaucracy. Ford's position is understandable. Coming to office on the heels

---

[12]President's Task Force on Governmental Organization, "The Organization and Management of Great Society Programs, Final Report of the President's Task Force on Governmental Organization," June 1967, p. 6. "Administratively confidential," unpublished.

[13]*Ibid.*, p. 1.

[14]Frederick C. Mosher and others, *Implications for Responsible Government*, prepared at the request of the Senate Select Committee on Presidential Campaign Activities by a panel of the National Academy of Public Administration (New York: Basic Books, Inc., 1974), p. 51.

of Watergate, in which the presidency as an institution had been dealt a hard blow, he was not in a position to exert aggressive leadership over the bureaucracy. Carter's situation is more complicated. His election can be attributed in part to his reputation as a manager and his claim of managerial prowess. Yet his management record as president was unimpressive. Carter's main contribution to the executive management tradition—an ironic one—was his successful effort to create a senior civil service system. The 1978 Civil Service Reform Act created a layer of top-level professionals in the career service with a new status enabling them to win bonuses and prizes for achievement, and also enabling their political superiors to move them around, or even to remove them from the senior service. The irony of this legislation lies in the fact that these new powers have been used aggressively by the Reagan administration to exert greater influence over the federal bureaucracy in order to pursue goals very different from Carter's.

THE ROLE OF THE BUREAUCRACY

The American federal bureaucracy, the object of presidential management control strategies, dates from 1883 when Congress passed the Pendleton Act in response to the assassination of President Garfield by a disappointed office seeker. Enactment of the Pendleton Act capped a thirty-year effort to replace the spoils system with a system for appointing career civil servants on the basis of merit.

The essential point of the civil-service reform movement was that elected officials should make policy and that professionals in the career service should carry it out. This notion, which implied that there could be a line of demarcation between policymaking and its execution, dominated theories of public administration, beginning in the 1920s. Although experts in this field have now abandoned the idea that such a line can be drawn to delineate the roles and responsibilities of political and career officials, there is still a strong, almost wistful, feeling on the part of some public administration specialists and old-line career officials that political officials should stay out of administrative processes.

Currently, the predominant view in political science is that the line between making and carrying out policy can never be clearly defined. This position holds that the point at which a political official's influence ends and a civil servant's responsibility begins varies with the issue at hand. It depends on the newness of the issue, the amount of money involved, and the level of public controversy generated. The last factor—*the level of public controversy*—is the most important one. Political scientist Paul H. Appleby observed thirty years ago, "The level at which a decision is made . . . may be shifted downward or upward as evaluations point to more or less controversy, or to more or less 'importance.' " [15]

AN ADMINISTRATIVE STRATEGY

Under an administrative presidency strategy a political executive should be just what the name indicates—*political and executive*. The basic premise is that management tasks *can and should* be performed by partisans. This concept is not only appropriate, but necessary, to a functioning democracy in a large and technologically advanced nation such as the United States.

Both Nixon and Reagan had important and legitimate policy objectives that, it is arguable, could best be carried out by administrative action—that is, by using the discretion permitted in the implementation of existing laws rather than advancing these policy aims through the enactment of new legislation. This is not to say that high-level political officials should perform detailed and routine management tasks. Quite the contrary. They can only operate on administrative matters if they are selective in their choice of issues and if they are actively supported by career officials in their agency. One of the most challenging relationships to work out is that between appointed officials and high-level professionals in the career service. Competence on the part of the career bureaucracy, as Hugh Heclo reminds us, requires that these officials be able to survive.[16] Ensuring that this will be so requires both sensitivity and political astuteness on the part of appointed officials in their relations with career officials.

THE NIXON EXPERIENCE

Richard Nixon stands out among recent presidents for the interest he took in administration. Actually, Nixon took two different approaches to administration in the field of domestic affairs in different periods of his presidency. When he entered office in 1969, Nixon emphasized the development of legislation that would put his stamp on domestic policy. White House working groups were set up to develop legislative initiatives in such fields as welfare, revenue sharing, education, health, urban affairs, the environment, and labor-management relations. In doing this, Nixon followed the pattern of his two immediate

---

[15]Paul H. Appleby, *Policy and Administration* (University, Ala.: University of Alabama Press, 1949), p. 13.

[16]For a discussion of this subject, see Hugh Heclo, *A Government of Strangers: Executive Politics in Washington* (Washington, D.C.: The Brookings Institution, 1977), Chapter 7.

predecessors, John F. Kennedy and Lyndon B. Johnson, each of whom had established a variety of legislative task forces.

Nixon also followed the lead of most of his predecessors in the criteria he used to select his cabinet members and the role he asked them to play at the beginning of his presidency. With two exceptions—Robert Finch at the Department of Health, Education, and Welfare and John Mitchell at the Department of Justice—the members of his cabinet were not close to Nixon personally, nor in some cases even politically. They represented a broad range of viewpoints, professions, and geographic areas. Several had gained national reputations before their appointments. This was especially true of the three former governors in Nixon's original cabinet—John Volpe of Massachusetts, secretary of transportation; George Romney of Michigan, secretary of housing and urban development; and Walter Hickel of Alaska, secretary of the interior.

In the first two years of Nixon's presidency, the White House focused on preparing new legislation—sometimes without the advice or even knowledge of the cabinet members whose departments would be affected. The secretaries of the domestic departments were essentially allowed to go their own way in selecting top program officials, supervising these officials, and handling other administrative tasks. For the most part, the White House staff concentrated its attention on Congress and its legislative agenda. Cabinet members heard from White House officials mostly in connection with legislative matters. This approach—which had been the traditional one—is called the *legislative strategy* in this book.

Gradually, however, the strategy shifted. The Nixon administration moved toward an administrative strategy. By the end of the first term, plans were made to shift the emphasis to the administrative approach for the second term. The legislative agenda was pared down. No longer was the cabinet to be composed of men with their own national standing disposed to go their own way. Unprecedented changes were made below the cabinet level. Trusted lieutenants who were tied personally to Richard Nixon and had no national reputations of their own were placed in direct charge of the major bureaucracies of domestic government. The goal in 1973, as Nixon's ill-fated second term got underway, was to take over the bureaucracy and by doing so to concentrate much more heavily on achieving policy objectives through administrative action.

The reason for Nixon's switch to an administrative strategy for his second term was the perception that the bureaucracy was a barrier to implementing his policies. This suspicion of the bureaucracy that motivated Nixon and his principal aides in 1972 and 1973 was not new to the political scene. From the very outset, the Nixon administration had been antibureaucracy. In part, this may have been a reflection of the fact that Republicans had been out of office for eight years under Johnson, just before Nixon's presidency. In part it reflected a

common attitude of suspicion on the part of conservatives toward big government. Such attitudes were not unfounded. It was true that many newly created
social programs of the Johnson period were staffed by career officials with a
commitment to the program area in which they worked.[17] Nixon staffers in
many of these cases were correct in assuming that this would produce opposition to their more conservative domestic policies and their efforts to achieve
decentralization.

The important difference was that, unlike many of its predecessors, the
Nixon administration did not come to terms with this initial attitude of mistrust of the bureaucracy or find ways to sublimate it, as had the Eisenhower
administration a decade earlier. On the contrary, these attitudes hardened to
the point that an unprecedented reorganization was put into place for Nixon's
second term to take control of the domestic bureaucracy.

Nixon's hostility toward the bureaucracy, almost vitriolic in its tone, was
apparent in many statements and actions. A White House aide in 1969 referred
to "the White House surrounded"—surrounded, that is, by powerful program
interests opposed to what the administration was trying to achieve. This attitude was also reflected in a suspicion in the early days of the career staff in the
Bureau of the Budget, now the Office of Management and Budget. It was not
dispelled until George Shultz replaced Nixon's first budget director, Robert
Mayo, who was regarded by the White House as too strong a defender of the
bureau's professionalism.[18] White House aide Michael Balzano summed up the
feelings of many in the Nixon inner circle about the federal bureaucracy.

> President Nixon doesn't run the bureaucracy; the civil service and the unions do. It
> took him three years to find out what was going on in the bureaucracy. And God
> forbid if any president is defeated after the first term, because then the bureauc-
> racy has another three years to play games with the next president.[19]

Even though hostility and suspicion underlaid Nixon's moves to trim the power
of the bureaucracy, his efforts raise more basic issues.

There are essentially three ways of viewing Nixon's decision in 1973 to
adopt an administrative presidency strategy for his second term. One is that he

---

[17]This point has been documented in Joel D. Aberbach and Bert A. Rochman. See "Clashing
Beliefs Within the Executive Bureaucracy: The Nixon Administration Bureaucracy," *The American Political Science Review*, vol. 70, no. 2, June 1976, pp. 456–468.

[18]In many respects Robert Mayo performed with wisdom and ability as President Nixon's
first budget director. Nevertheless, his lack of experience in political matters made it difficult for
him to build confidence in the bureau on the part of the president and the White House at the outset of an administration that followed an eight-year Republican hiatus. Mayo tangled most with
John Ehrlichman, who engineered his sudden and, to Mayo, completely unexpected removal in the
middle of 1970.

[19]As quoted in the *Wall Street Journal*, June 21, 1972.

was right. A second is that he was partly right—that in a pluralistic society, many forces can and should influence the bureaucracy, including (but not limited to) the president. The difference between the first and second position is one of degree. The essential question is: What should be the role of the elected chief executive in relation to other power centers in influencing the professional staff of executive branch agencies? One can argue that the Congress, the courts, interest groups, the press, etc., ought to be as influential as the chief executive, or even more.

The argument in this book is that the political chief executives—which includes the president, governors, mayors—should have *the most important role* in this area of modern government. Purely as a practical matter, the chief executive is in a much better position than a large group of people in a legislative body or the courts to give cohesive policy direction and guidance to the work of large public bureaucracies.

There is still a third possible way to view the role of elected officials, which this book rejects—that elected chief executives should have a limited role in the administrative process. This position concedes that there is a substantial policy content to many administrative processes, but argues that policymaking in modern government is a proper responsibility of career or professional bureaucrats. Peter Woll, for example, portrays the federal bureaucracy as "an independent force." He says it "cannot be dismissed simply as a part of the executive branch of government controlled by the president or the cabinet."[20] Woll depicts the bureaucracy as a "a powerful and viable branch of government, playing a political game to advance its own interest in legislative and judicial, as well as executive matters." Although it is long, it is useful here to include a section of Woll's views on what he calls "the political nature of bureaucracy."

> The political nature of bureaucracy is initially revealed in the behavior of administrative agencies acting as interest groups and in individual behavior within administrative agencies. Administrative agencies come into contact with various external groups both governmental and non-government. To retain their power or to expand all agencies must maintain a balance of political support over opposition. Congress controls finances and has ultimate power over reorganization; thus the agencies always seek political support that can be exerted on Congress. They are responsive to the president, or his coordinating staff agencies such as the Bureau of the Budget, only insofar as they are essential to the maintenance of political support. Agencies that have strong interest group support outside the bureaucracy do not generally have to rely on the president or his staff agencies. On the other hand, some agencies without adequate outside group support must substitute presidential support

---

[20]Peter Woll, *The American Bureaucracy* (New York: W.W. Norton & Co., 1963), p. 3. A similar view of the role of the bureaucracy in contemporary government is expressed in Francis E. Rourke, *Bureaucracy, Politics, and Public Policy* (Boston: Little, Brown, 1969).

in order to survive. One important determinant of presidential control over any particular administrative agency is the extent of the agency's contact with and support from private interest groups. The effectiveness of this control, of course, will vary with the power of the private groups concerned and their ability to influence Congress or the Courts.[21]

An even stronger statement of this point of view has been expressed by Norton Long.[22] Writing thirty years ago, Long argued that we should not only accept the bureaucracy for what it is, but we should strive to make the bureaucracy independent. This should be so, according to Long, because the bureaucracy represents not just special interests, but the whole nation better than any other of our political institutions. Based on what he calls "our working constitution," Long contends that the bureaucracy has a substantial role as a "representative organ and source of rationality." The bureaucracy is "our great fourth branch of government." There should be, Long argues, a working interaction of the four, not the legal supremacy of any of them.

THE REAGAN EXPERIENCE

Nixon's administrative presidency approach to the relationship between political officials and the bureaucracy was the subject of a book I wrote in 1974, titled *The Plot that Failed: Nixon and the Administrative Presidency.* The book grew out of my observations while serving in the U.S. Office of Management and Budget (part of the Executive Office of the President) during Nixon's first term. It raised the question of whether the president should try to exert more influence over the bureaucracy, but did not really answer it. I found it hard then to clear away the resentment I felt that the hard work of the men and women who had served in policy positions in the Nixon administration was being destroyed by the backwash of the Watergate scandal.

In the intervening years, I kept coming back to the questions raised by Nixon's administrative presidency strategy. I have now come to the conclusion that, while his motives may not have been as pure as the driven snow, Nixon was right in deciding to adopt an administrative strategy in 1973. The experience of the Reagan presidency in the management arena led to my decision to update and extend my work on the role of the president as a manager of the bureaucracy in the field of domestic affairs.

The Reagan administration came to office with a strong commitment to retrenchment and to reducing the size and scope of government in domestic affairs. Whether one agrees with this objective or not, there is a question here for

[21]Woll, *op. cit.*, p. 4.

[22]See Norton E. Long, "Bureaucracy and Constitutionalism," *The American Political Science Review*, vol. 46, no. 3, September 1952, p. 808.

democratic government involving its ability to respond to changes in basic social values.

What caught my attention as the Reagan administration got under way was its *dual approach* to domestic affairs, involving *both* legislative and administrative actions to curtail the government's spending and reduce its role in domestic affairs. The interesting aspect of this dual strategy is its administrative dimension.

The lessons of the Nixon period and the frustrations of the Carter presidency have produced a body of experience that the Reagan White House has drawn on skillfully in attempting to push its influence into the administrative processes of government. A *Wall Street Journal* article, written a year after Reagan took office, said his administration "has found a way to reshape the federal government without necessarily changing laws. It is called Reaganizing."[23] The article went on to define Reaganizing as "the transformation of departments and agencies by appointed officials devoted to President Reagan's vow to 'curb the size and influence of the federal establishment.' "

The Reagan administrative strategy is different from Nixon's in a number of respects. It went into effect earlier, right at the beginning of the Reagan presidency. It is less visible and more subtle. It focuses more at the subcabinet level. It is less regimented than the Nixon plan, which was dramatically announced at the outset of the second term as Nixon shifted gears from the conventional legislative approach to an administrative strategy. The biggest difference between Reagan and Nixon is that the Reagan administration has pursued a dual approach to domestic affairs, whereas Nixon started out with one approach (legislative) and then switched to another (administrative).

A major feature of this book is the comparison of the Nixon and Reagan administrative strategies. Chapters 2 through 4 on the Nixon period draw heavily on my earlier book. Chapters 5 and 6 discuss the Reagan experience. Both the section on Nixon and the new section on the Reagan presidency begin with a discussion of the substance of domestic policy, and then explore tactics—both administrative and legislative. Chapter 7 summarizes lessons learned from the Nixon and Reagan experiences and those of other recent presidents. Major documents on the domestic policies and administrative tactics of the two administrations are presented in the final section.

BASIC ISSUES EXAMINED

Examining Nixon's and Reagan's administrative tactics can help us to understand fundamental issues of American governance. As government in the United States has become larger and more specialized, experts have come to ex-

---

[23]Schorr and Pasztor, *op. cit.*, p. 1.

ert growing influence. According to Max Weber, bureaucratic organization involves "the exercise of control on the basis of knowledge."[24] Writing at the turn of the century, Weber viewed bureaucratic control as inevitably increasing as scientific expertise expands. The dilemma of bureaucratic centralization for democratic government is the obvious one. The idea that citizens through their representatives should make governmental decisions is not consistent with a system in which decisions about public policy frequently are made on the basis of technical knowledge.

In the mid-1930s, E. Pendleton Herring wrote about this dilemma in discussing the "increase in administrative discretion." Referring to the role of the administrator, Herring wrote: "The words of the statute delimit his scope, but within the margin of his discretion he must write his interpretation of state purpose." The result, said Herring, is "the transfer from Congress [to the bureaucracy] of much of the direct superintendence of reconciling the conflicting groups within the state."[25]

In this context, the idea of an administrative presidency strategy can be seen as reinforcing democratic theory. The disillusionment with government in the current period should increase the appeal of politicians who have as a major purpose *making government work better.* Doing so requires that *politics penetrate* operations, that the values politicians are elected to advance are reflected in the execution of laws, as well as in their enactment.[26] An important fact that has already been mentioned is critical at this juncture in the argument, specifically, the large and growing amount of administrative discretion contained in the laws of modern governments.

The argument that politics should penetrate operations applies both to liberal and conservative political agendas. Although both of the presidents discussed in this volume (Reagan particularly) are conservatives, the need to adopt an administrative strategy is just as strong, if not stronger in the current period, for liberal chief executives. The 1980s ushered in what undoubtedly will be a long period of austerity in U.S. domestic affairs. If liberals are to respond to this new reality, they must be able to demonstrate that government can work, that rigor and efficiency can be brought to bear to solve social problems. The next liberal agenda has to be one that gives greater weight than in the past to the capability of governmental institutions to carry out social purposes.

[24]See Max Weber, *The Theory of Social and Economic Organization* (Glencoe, Ill.: The Free Press, 1947).

[25]E. Pendleton Herring, *Public Administration and the Public Interest* (New York: McGraw-Hill Book Co., 1936), p. 8.

[26]This same argument is made, although somewhat wistfully, in a recent book by two writers who worked in the Carter administration. See Ben W. Heineman, Jr., and Curtis A. Hessler, *Memorandum for the President: A Strategic Approach to Domestic Affairs in the 1980s* (New York: Random House, 1980).

To summarize, both theory and practice are shifting on the role of politicians in administrative processes. This book draws primarily on the Nixon and Reagan experience to study the rationale for, and workings of, an administrative strategy on the part of political officials. I have updated the Nixon analysis and have added, although not in as much detail, material about Reagan, as well as other presidents. The main purpose of the new edition is not to be descriptive, but to argue a point: *It is desirable and right for politicians to become more involved in administrative processes.* The point has been made by others, and was made by me—though less clearly—in the earlier version of this study. André Gide in *The Return of the Prodigal*, said, "Everything has already been told, but as no one listens, we must begin again." The idea of an administrative presidency strategy is important enough to be treated again.

CHAPTER 2

Nixon's Domestic Agenda

Before examining the management tactics of a particular president in the field of domestic affairs, we must examine the substance. For the Nixon administration, a close relationship exists between what Richard Nixon sought to achieve in the area of domestic policy and the tactics he ultimately adopted. As his policy goals became more fully spelled out, the management approach, involving tighter controls over the domestic bureaucracy, came to be viewed within the Nixon White House as the most promising technique for achieving his domestic policy goals.

1968 CAMPAIGN THEMES

In the 1968 campaign, Richard Nixon's speeches and statements on domestic affairs reflected little of substance and hardly any specificity. But even though his statements were general, as is customary on the stump, his main points were hard-hitting. Repeatedly, Nixon criticized the domestic record of the Kennedy and Johnson administrations. He complained that the federal government did not deliver, that new domestic programs were overly ambitious and expensive, and that social problems were not reduced accordingly. Nixon stressed the need to change the basic relationship between the federal government and states and localities. In September 1968 he said, "For years now, the trend has been to sweep more and more authority toward Washington. Too many decisions that would better have been made in Seattle or St. Louis have wound up on the president's desk."[1]

Nixon's campaign themes in 1968 for domestic policy involved more than shifting power away from Washington. He discussed his views in a manner that appeared to anticipate proposals he would later make as president. He argued for a stronger federal role in those areas of domestic affairs that he contended required national action. Nixon said that one of his main purposes in decentralizing power would be "to concentrate federal action on those functions that can only be handled at the federal level."[2]

These phrases and ideas were standard for centrists, pragmatic politicians, like Nixon, in the 1960s and gradually were adopted by persons of other political viewpoints. Dissatisfaction with the performance of the federal government in domestic affairs was widespread, although there was little agreement on what should be done about it. George Wallace, governor of Alabama, who ran as a conservative-independent candidate for president in 1968, disparaged briefcase-toting federal bureaucrats. He vigorously challenged the response of traditional liberals that new domestic problems required national governmental solutions.

This was a prominent theme for conservative Republicans in the 1960s. Although it had been expressed without much success in Senator Barry Goldwater's 1964 bid for the presidency, Goldwater's conservative and decentralist philosophy became increasingly more acceptable. After the 1966 congressional elections, in which Republicans achieved important gains, Republican members of Congress stepped up their attacks on the basic premises of Lyndon Johnson's Great Society that the federal government should intervene forcefully in many areas of social affairs.

Liberals, too, were changing their view on the appropriate role of the federal government. Revenue sharing, a new approach to domestic policy intended to strengthen the role of state and local governments, was advocated in both major party platforms in 1968.

Senator Robert Kennedy reflected this shift in opinion among liberals on domestic issues. In his campaign for the 1968 Democratic nomination, Kennedy developed his ideas on domestic policy along lines that bore a striking resemblance to what many Republicans were saying in this period.[3] In Utah in March he told a college audience, "We must return control to the people themselves" and went so far as to suggest a reversal of his brother's New Frontier policies.

---

[1]Radio Address, September 19, 1968.
[2]*Ibid.*
[3]Robert Kennedy was shot by an assassin on June 5, 1968, and died the following day.

In the last analysis it should be in the cities and towns and villages where the decisions are made not in Washington. . . . Solutions of the 1930s are not the solutions of today. The solutions of the New Frontier, of the early 1960s are not necessarily applicable now. We are a new generation with new problems.[4]

There was also growing sentiment among radical groups in the late 1960s that resembled the views of many politicians. Leaders of the New Left demanding "power to the people" flailed away at national bureaucracies in much the same way that conservative politicians, and some liberals, won applause by criticizing governmental paternalism and heavy-handedness.

NIXON'S DOMESTIC PROGRAM EMERGES

Nixon moved quickly after the 1968 election to set up machinery in the White House for domestic policymaking. As one of his first acts, he established an Urban Affairs Council. To direct the group, he brought in Daniel Patrick Moynihan, a creative iconoclast on the Democratic side among intellectuals (and now Democratic senator from New York). At the first meeting of the council on January 23, 1969, Nixon called on the group to work out new approaches. He said the first few months of a new administration are the time for change and warned the group against acquiring a vested interest in program failures. Nixon charged his advisers to develop a bold program of reform so that in later years people could not accuse them of being too cautious.

The program eventually adopted by the Nixon administration involved restructuring the two dominant types of federal domestic programs: (1) grants-in-aid, under which assistance is provided to state and local governments, and (2) income-transfer programs, through which assistance is provided to needy individuals. Together, these two types of programs account for most nondefense federal expenditures.

The first major statement of Nixon's plans came August 8, 1969, in a television address to the nation in which he first used the phrase "New Federalism."[5] The origins of the New Federalism address are interesting.

During the period from Nixon's inauguration until August 8, 1969, the business of domestic policymaking had dragged out longer than the president wanted. Many protracted meetings had been held on program details and techniques. This was especially true of welfare reform, which at every turn became more difficult and complex than had been originally anticipated. The president

---

[4]John Herbers, "Kennedy to Enter Indiana's Primary," *New York Times*, March 28, 1968, p. 1.

[5]See Document 1.

was impatient. Early in July he instructed press secretary Ronald Ziegler to state publicly that his domestic program would be announced in the first week of August right after the president returned from an overseas trip. The die was cast, and in this case the deadline was met. (On other occasions Nixon was less successful in using this technique of publicly setting a deadline for a particular action to try to force his advisers to have it ready by that time.)

Nixon's August 8 address on domestic policy, aired in prime evening time, laid out the philosophy of his program and presented four specific proposals—welfare reform, revenue sharing,[6] a new manpower training act, and the reorganization of the Office of Economic Opportunity, which operated the "war on poverty" program initiated under President Johnson. The domestic program was well received. An article in the *London Economist*, August 16, 1969, stated:

> It is no exaggeration to say that President Nixon's television message on welfare reform and revenue sharing may rank in importance with President Roosevelt's first proposal for a social security system in the mid-1930s. . . .

The article concluded:

> the chances are that most men, and most members of Congress, will in the end see that these major reforms are right for this time in this country.

Other press accounts were also enthusiastic. The *San Francisco Chronicle* said of the president's welfare proposal:

> the Nixon measure has the great advantages of being not only "noble in purpose" but also suited to the needs of the day and the will of the people.

The *New York Daily News* commented:

> Revenue sharing would be a giant step in the direction of dismantling the cumbersome apparatus that has grown up in Washington. It can't happen too soon to suit us.

The *Christian Science Monitor* called the president's program overall "a major watershed—socially, economically," and politically.

---

[6]Revenue sharing turned out to be the most conspicuous legislative achievement of the Nixon administration in domestic affairs. Appropriately, it went into effect just before Christmas in 1972 and involved the distribution of $30.2 billion to 38,600 states, counties, townships, cities, and Indian tribes over a period of five years. For further information on revenue sharing, see Richard P. Nathan, Allen D. Manvel, Susannah E. Calkins, and associates, *Monitoring Revenue Sharing* (Washington, D.C.: The Brookings Institution, 1975).

The most dramatic component of Nixon's New Federalism was his family assistance plan for welfare reform. Although revenue sharing and two of the major block grants proposed by Nixon (for community development and employment and training) were enacted, the family assistance plan was not.

SORTING OUT FUNCTIONS

The key concept of the Nixon domestic program was the need to sort out and rearrange responsibilities among the federal, state, and local governments and between the public and private sectors. Nixon's program called for decentralizing some governmental programs and at the same time centralizing others where it was felt to be appropriate for the national government to have principal responsibility. Although the criteria were not systematic as in an academic treatise, for a political program Nixon's brand of New Federalism was quite coherent.

Functions to be decentralized were primarily those involving services provided in the community, that is, where government itself manages an activity. Typically, these are services for which conditions and needs vary among communities and where local decision making was felt to be especially important. Examples are education, social services for the poor, manpower training, urban and rural community development, and law enforcement. The people who provide these services are organized differently from one community to another.

On the other hand, the functions of government for which greater national responsibility was advocated by the Nixon administration include three main types:

1. Those for which the benefits of government action *spill over* from one area to another. An example is protection of the environment.
2. Those that involve *transfers* (both of cash and of in-kind services) to individuals. In this area, national action ensures that benefits are uniform throughout the country. Examples are social security, welfare, and health insurance.
3. Those for which a *stimulus* or *demonstration effect* is desirable. Drug abuse prevention is an example of a new program established for this purpose in the Nixon period.

All of these areas were identified by the Nixon administration as candidates for central governmental action.

Nixon often referred to the need to sort out and rationalize domestic governmental functions. In a memorandum to senior administration officials urging them to support revenue sharing in June 1970, he explained his New Federalism program in the following terms.

Under the New Federalism, major aims are to define more clearly functional responsibilities among levels of government and strengthen governmental institutions at all levels. Welfare, for example, is appropriately a national responsibility.

This statement continued:

In areas which are primarily State-local responsibilities, revenue sharing and other measures which the Administration has advanced will strengthen the capacity of States and localities to make decisions which reflect their own priorities and needs.

The president made the same point in his 1971 state of the union message:[7]

Established functions that are clearly and essentially Federal in nature will still be performed by the Federal Government. New functions that need to be sponsored or performed by the Federal Government—such as those I have urged tonight in welfare and health—will be added to the Federal agenda. Whenever it makes the best sense for us to act as a whole nation, the Federal Government should and will lead the way. But where State or local governments can better do what needs to be done, let us see that they have the resources to do it there.

As Nixon and his aides became more familiar with domestic programs, the administration's statements contained more specific ideas on the distinction between federal or state-local responsibilities. Speaking extemporaneously about the environment in a February 1970 address at the National Governors' Conference in Washington, Nixon explained his ideas on the relationship between revenue sharing and national initiatives for environmental protection in the following terms:

When we look at the problem of the environment and where we go, there are these thoughts I would like to leave with you: first the necessity that the approach be national. I believe in States' responsibilities. This is why revenue sharing to me is a concept that should be adopted. On the other hand, when we consider the problem of the environment it is very clear that clean air and clean water doesn't stop at a State line. And it is also very clear that if one State adopts very stringent regulations, it has the effect of penalizing itself as against another State which has regulations which are not as stringent insofar as attracting the private enterprise that might operate in one State or another or that might make that choice. That is why we have suggested national standards.[8]

Similarly, the administration over time developed an increasingly more

---

[7]See Document 2.

[8]President's Remarks, Winter Session of the National Governors' Conference in Washington, D.C., February 27, 1970.

specific position on the appropriateness of national responsibility for income-transfer programs. In a message to the Congress on welfare in March 1972, the president said that the welfare-payment function is appropriately a national responsibility.

> While decentralized management is highly desirable in many fields and is indeed central to my philosophy of government, I believe that many of these problems in welfare administration can best be solved by using a national automated payments system, which would produce economies and considerably increase both equity of treatment and tighten administration.[9]

The president in the same message stressed that under his plan, "States and counties would be freed to concentrate on social services to recipients, making use of their closer understanding of the needs of local residents."[10] This distinction between activities like the transfer-payment function as national and social services as state-local was the central tenet of the Nixon brand of New Federalism.

REVENUE SHARING

The instruments for decentralization under Nixon were of two types—what Nixon called "*general* revenue sharing" and "*special* revenue sharing." "General revenue sharing" refers to money provided to state and local governments on an essentially unconditional basis. In his first year in office, Nixon proposed $500 million per year for this purpose. The congressional response, however, was tepid. Two years later, with this legislation languishing in Congress, Nixon upped the ante tenfold, recommending $5 billion per year for general revenue sharing.[11] The new bill, as expected, activated the lobbying groups for state and local governments, and the legislation began to move. It was enacted in the fall of 1972. Nixon signed the revenue sharing act in a ceremony in Independence Hall in Philadelphia October 20, 1972, in the presence of a large group of state and local officials. He expressed his hope that revenue sharing would "renew the American federal system created in Philadelphia two centuries earlier."

[9]Presidential Message, March 27, 1972. In the welfare area, in particular, the Nixon administration's support for increased federal control cooled toward the end of the first term. However, the adult welfare categories (aged, blind, and disabled) were federalized under the aegis of the Social Security Administration in 1972. These three groups accounted for nearly half of the caseload of state and county welfare agencies in 1972.

[10]President's Remarks, Winter Session of the National Governors' Conference in Washington, D.C., February 27, 1970.

[11]See Document 2.

"Special revenue sharing," the other main instrument for decentralization under Nixon, refers to grants to state and local governments provided in broad functional areas—community development, education, employment and training, law enforcement, and social services—with relatively few conditions attached. This term "special revenue sharing" never caught on, and was eventually dropped. The earlier designation of "block grants" was reinstated and continues to be used. The basic idea is that block grants are more flexible than "categorical" grants, which had been a major instrument of Johnson's Great Society but were a source of continued criticism. Economist Walter Heller, chairman of the Council of Economic Advisors under Kennedy and one of the early supporters of the revenue sharing idea, used as an argument for revenue sharing the problem caused by what he called *"the hardening of the categories."*

Of the six "special revenue sharing" proposals advanced by Nixon, two were for human-resource services and the other four were for community development. Thus, the organization of the New Federalism can be summarized according to four functional areas. Human-resource services and community development programs were designated as appropriate areas for decentralization initiatives, whereas in the fields of income security and natural resources (which include environmental programs such as air and water pollution control) the proposals advanced by the Nixon administration involved increased central governmental responsibility.

In examining areas selected for decentralization, it is important to keep an additional distinction in mind. Government programs can be divided into three main aspects: (1) financing, (2) policymaking, and (3) administration. For functions to be decentralized under Nixon's brand of New Federalism, the federal government would continue to help finance many of these activities through general or special revenue sharing. These broader and less conditional federal-aid instruments would permit greater scope to states and localities for the other two aspects of a government program—policymaking and administration.

WELFARE REFORM

Welfare reform was the biggest surprise of Nixon's domestic program. Nixon in his 1968 campaign talked in conventional terms about the need to overhaul welfare and "build bridges to human dignity." Yet he had never in his previous career evidenced a strong or specific interest in this area.

Nixon's advocacy of welfare reform—notably his family assistance plan proposed in August 1969—can be viewed on three levels. On the first level, the president had pledged himself to improve the government's performance in ar-

"What a novel idea. Applying it to the poor, too."

(Sanders in *The Milwaukee Journal*. Courtesy Field Newspaper Syndicate.)

eas where it was falling down. Welfare was an obvious candidate. Public discontent was widespread with the major federally assisted welfare categories.[12]

On the second level, Nixon's family assistance plan can be considered as part of the administration's larger effort to sort out governmental functions in domestic affairs and assign to the federal level those responsibilities best suited for central action on a basis that assures that the federal government will do

[12]The four categories of federally assisted welfare programs in 1969 when Nixon took office were aid for the aged, blind, disabled, and the most troubled category of all, aid to families with dependent children (AFDC). Costs and caseloads under AFDC were rising rapidly in the 1960s. Total costs doubled from January 1960 to 1969; caseloads rose in that period from 5.8 to 9.3 million. Many welfare systems had severe administrative problems. Administrative costs were high; almost 20 cents out of every dollar of AFDC spending in 1968 went for administration. Recipients, too, were discontented. Payment levels in many jurisdictions were very low—$7 per family per month under AFDC in Mississippi, as compared to ten times that amount in some states. All of these conditions changed in the 1970s. Caseload growth under AFDC has almost stopped; administrative systems have been improved; and interstate disparities in benefit levels of AFDC payments and food stamps combined have been markedly reduced.

the job properly. The argument was made for Nixon's family assistance plan that the administration of automated payment systems for assisting individuals based on need uniformly throughout the nation is appropriately a central government responsibility. The obvious precedent was social security.

The third level of analysis contains a note of irony. Philosophically, welfare reform is an extension of decentralization. Nixon's plan for welfare reform involved reducing the government's efforts to solve the problems of the poor through social services in favor of having the poor, who receive cash assistance, solve their own problems. Nixon emphasized this point in an address to the White House Conference on Food, Nutrition, and Health on December 2, 1969. He said that the administration's policies for improving the living conditions of the poor are based on a simple proposition; "that the best judge of each family's priorities is that family itself; that the best way to ameliorate the hardships of poverty is to provide the family with additional income—to be spent as that family sees fit."[13] This is called "the income strategy."

> The task for Government is not to make decisions for you or for anyone. The task of Government is to enable you to make decisions for yourselves. Not to see the truth of that statement is fundamentally to mistake the genius of democracy. We have made too many mistakes of this type—but no more. Our job is to get resources to people in need and then to let them run their own lives.[14]

The history of welfare reform under Nixon reflects the shifts and permutations of his domestic program. White House strategists blew hot and cold on welfare. In 1972, when Democratic presidential candidate George McGovern offered a controversial national proposal for a guaranteed income in his California primary campaign, Nixon pulled back his support from his family assistance plan in order not to deflect criticism from McGovern or diminish its strength and standing. Two years later in his state of the union message, Nixon appeared to come back to the fold, promising what sounded like an even broader version of his original plan. Other events, however, interceded. Welfare reform legislation was never reintroduced.

In retrospect, it is just as well that Nixon never advanced (nor did Gerald Ford) the welfare plan being developed in 1974.[15] This new version of the family assistance plan would have resulted in *lower* benefits for large numbers of beneficiaries. Moreover, it had no real chance of enactment, and would have undercut the enactment of desirable, smaller changes in welfare programs. A new approach calling for less sweeping "incremental" changes in welfare of-

---

[13]Presidential Address, White House Conference on Food, Nutrition, and Health, December 2, 1969. This speech was the high point of Moynihan's influence in the Nixon White House.

[14]*Ibid*.

[15]See Document 6.

fered more promise in 1974. Although the national government took over responsibility for welfare for the aged and disabled in 1972 under Nixon (this was
part of his overall welfare reform plan), the most controversial welfare program—AFDC for working-age adults with children—continues to be structured on a basis that assigns major responsibility to the states.[16]

SHIFTING PRIORITIES

On an overall basis, there was a substantial increase in spending for human-resource programs during the Nixon presidency. This was especially true of income transfers, that is, payments to individuals, both in the form of cash and
so-called in-kind benefits, such as food stamps, medical care, and housing.
In his message accompanying the budget for fiscal year 1971—the first budget
for which he was fully responsible—Nixon emphasized that spending on all human-resource programs in that year would for the first time exceed spending
on defense. This was the turning point. Four years later, when Nixon's fiscal
year 1975 budget proposal was presented, payments to individuals alone far ex-
ceeded defense, having almost doubled in cost in that period. Total spending
for payments to individuals in fiscal 1975 (including social security) accounted
for nearly half of the entire federal budget, as shown in Table 2-1.[17]

**Table 2–1   Composition of Federal Budget Outlays, Selected Years
(in billions of dollars)**

Type of Spending	1969		1971		1975	
	Amount	*Percent*	*Amount*	*Percent*	*Amount*	*Percent*
Defense	79.4	43	75.8	36	85.6	26
Human resources	63.3	34	88.5	42	166.8	51
Payments to individuals	55.3	30	78.7	37	150.4	46
Other	8.0	4	9.8	5	16.4	5
Interest	12.7	7	14.8	7	23.2	7
Other	28.2	15	31.0	15	48.7	15
Total	183.6	10	210.2	100	324.2	100

Source: Federal Government Finances, 1983 Budget Data, Tables 9 and 10, February 1982.

[16]Ronald Reagan's plan to turn over full responsibility for AFDC to the states is discussed in
Chapter 5.

[17]Not all of this increase was deliberate. Much of it was attributable to social security increases that Nixon signed, although reluctantly. Many of the same conditions applied to medicare
and medicaid. Nevertheless, Nixon's advocacy of programs in this area (food stamps, health insurance, family assistance, and an automatic escalator for social security) influenced this program
growth materially.

REFLECTIONS ON THE NIXON AGENDA FOR DOMESTIC AFFAIRS

Nixon's domestic program cannot be summarized as conservative, centrist, or progressive. Its tone and emphasis changed as political conditions changed. In the early days and on the heels of a close election, the domestic program had a quite progressive cast. Helping the poor, not catching the welfare cheats, was the theme of the family assistance plan. This subject absorbed the largest amount of time and energy among domestic policy proposals in the early days of the first term. George Shultz, as secretary of labor, was particularly influential in this period. He was able to win Nixon over to a quite liberal civil rights plan, the so-called Philadelphia Plan, for the construction industry. The Philadelphia Plan involved quotas (called "targets") for hiring minorities. It was strongly opposed by organized labor.

The sharpest among many shifts in Nixon's domestic program came at the end of the first term and just after the president's reelection, with the swing in this case being hard to the right. Nixon's posture on domestic issues shifted back toward center one year later in 1974 as the idea of impeachment gained strength in the Congress. However, these shifts and permutations (and there were a number of them) did not mean that the basic approach of the Nixon administration changed each time. The tone and emphasis changed, and so did proposed spending levels, but the basic framework of the administration's domestic program was not affected. In fact, the major aims of Nixon's domestic program remained surprisingly constant. The combined effect of the enactment of general revenue sharing in 1972, the employment and training block grant in 1973, and the community development block grant in 1974, along with the dramatic increases in income transfers and the relative decline in the importance of categorical grants for social services constituted an appreciable change from Lyndon Johnson's Great Society.

Nixon's domestic policies involved other legislative and budgetary proposals aside from those highlighted here, of course. This chapter merely presents a framework and suggests that in many ways and in many areas this program was rooted in important social values and reflected, although in varying degrees in different periods, a concern for the individual, the community, and the needs of the poor. The Nixon first term, it should be remembered, achieved success in many areas. If for some reason Richard Nixon had not stood for reelection, it is interesting to reflect on how history might have treated his accomplishments. There is reason to think he would have been given a high ranking. His large margin in 1972 supports such a conclusion. Moreover, many of the men and women who worked hard on Nixon's domestic program would by most accounts be credited as distinguished and able—Shultz, Richardson, Moynihan, Burns, to name a few, and a large number of talented men and women in the next line of policy positions.

From the point of view of the federal bureaucracy, however, the essential implications of Nixon's brand of New Federalism are clear. *The idea was to weaken the federal bureaucracy.* This, in fact, is likely to be the outcome of any strategy involving significant governmental decentralization and an "income strategy" to aid the poor. Just as in physics, when political power is given to one group (in this case state and local governments and individuals), it must be taken away from someone else. In seeking to enhance the role of states and localities and to give greater opportunity to the poor to make their own decisions, Nixon's policies involved taking power away from specialized bureaucracies of the federal government. At the outset this strategy was not generally perceived in these terms. However, tensions between the White House and the bureaucracy grew rapidly as Nixon's domestic policies were spelled out. Increasingly, and as a logical outgrowth of these policies, the Nixon presidency was marked by animosity between the White House and the domestic bureaucracy.

CHAPTER 3

Relations Between the White House and Agencies in Nixon's First Term

Once a president's domestic policy has taken form, what does he do to put it into effect? The best way to begin to understand Richard Nixon's plans for implementing his domestic program is to examine the relationship between the White House and the people named to head the departments and agencies of the federal executive establishment.

THE ROLE OF CABINET OFFICERS

Coming into office in 1969, Nixon approached cabinet making in the traditional manner, naming a representative group of men who could win approval as a panel of distinguished citizens. On December 11, 1968, he took an unprecedented step, going on national television to introduce the cabinet *en bloc*. The president-elect introduced each member separately and stated his qualifications. He concluded by saying, "Every one of these men that I have introduced to you is an *independent thinker.*"[1] He added:

> I don't want a Cabinet of "Yes" men and I don't think you want a Cabinet of "Yes" men. Every man in the Cabinet will be urged to speak out in Cabinet and within the Administration on all the great issues so that the decisions we will make will be the best decisions we can possibly reach.[2]

[1]Remarks of President-elect Richard M. Nixon, "Announcing Nominations of Cabinet Members," The Shoreham Hotel, Washington, D.C., December 11, 1968. Italics added.
[2]*Ibid.*

At this point, Nixon's management philosophy, if he had one at all, was not revealed beyond some general statements to the effect that he wanted "independent thinkers [who will] . . . speak out . . . on all the great issues."

In this respect, Nixon was no different from many other politicians. Most are trained as legislators, operating in the give-and-take of lawmaking, with only a small staff under their direct supervision. Having been defeated in his bid for governor of California in 1962, Nixon had never been directly responsible for a large organization. His notion of management in 1969 seemed to be that it was a profession or science, that expert managers from the business world could improve the performance and efficiency of the government, but that it was not an area of direct presidential responsibility and action.

Nixon's view was different from that of most experts in public administration. The dominant public administration theory on the presidency (a view that Nixon later embraced) advocates a strong role for the president as a manager of the executive branch. Two strategies for strengthening presidential management have been advocated and used over the years: (1) expanding and upgrading the president's executive office staff, and (2) relying on strengthened cabinet officers who are explicitly assigned responsibility for management.

Despite the surface appeal of combining these two approaches, the experience of the Nixon years clearly demonstrates that these two strategies do not go together. A strong White House staff interested in managing the executive branch is likely to weaken the role of the cabinet officer and *vice versa*. The president must choose between these two management strategies. This was not recognized at the outset of the Nixon administration—in fact, it is still not very well understood. Later, when the need to choose between the two strategies became apparent to Nixon, he first decided in favor of a strong White House staff and then in favor of strong cabinet officers. The story of this shift is in large measure the management story of the Nixon presidency.

PRESSURES ON THE CABINET SECRETARY

Although Nixon in 1968 said he wanted strong cabinet officers, events in the earliest days of his administration caused him to change his mind. The change is very much in keeping with what had been written about the role of the cabinet officer, though the Nixon inner circle showed little evidence of knowledge of this literature. Cabinet members are often viewed as *advocates* for agency interests rather than as *spokesmen* for the president. This advocacy role often leads to an adversarial relationship with the president as cabinet members advocate policies that are inconsistent with the overall policy framework developed by the White House. This adversarial relationship dominated the first term of the Nixon administration for three major reasons.

One reason was that Nixon's original cabinet had been named to *represent* major interests in the inner councils of government. Cabinet members in many instances were named to serve two masters—external groups and interests and, in addition, what might be called the internal needs of the president. George Romney, for example, came to the cabinet as the man who would speak for liberal Republicans and for the needs of the nation's cities. The same applied to Nixon's first secretary of agriculture, Clifford Hardin. In announcing his cabinet choices on December 11, 1969, Nixon described Hardin as a "man who could speak eloquently *for* farmers, for rural America, and agriculture *to* the president."[3]

Preidentification with a given program or viewpoint is not the only reason a cabinet member becomes a spokesman *to* rather than *for* the president. Forces that come into play after a person is appointed also pull new appointees into the orbit of the program interests of their agency. Nixon's cabinet and sub-cabinet appointees began their term of office with an almost ritualistic courting and mating process with the bureaucracy. On the advice of career agency officials, and by their own choosing, they were closeted for long hours in orientation sessions with program officials who "explained" to them the goals and accomplishments of the programs they had inherited. It soon became clear to many of the new appointees that these experts would be needed close at hand to supply facts about complex programs and to help shape policy initiatives. In many obvious and subtle ways, the respect of the agency's permanent staff depended on the performance of the new presidential appointees as a spokesman *for* the agency's interests. John Ehrlichman, who eventually became the chief domestic policy aide to Nixon, remarked at a press briefing late in 1972 that after the administration appointed key officials to high posts and they had their picture taken with the president, "We only see them at the annual White House Christmas party; they go off and marry the natives."

These co-option pressures were a major factor in the difficulties with the White House experienced by Robert Finch as secretary of health, education, and welfare (HEW). Long a close aide of Nixon's, Finch had serious problems reconciling his new role as the leader of a complex and costly array of social programs with his personal ties to the president, who had reservations about many of these programs. In introducing Finch on December 11, 1968, the president-elect specifically said that "he will not simply add billions to programs that have failed, but would find new ways to solve social problems."[4]

Finch could not seem to pull away from the liberal staff of HEW who demanded that he speak for them. Tensions on this score continued throughout Finch's stormy eighteen months as secretary. In the midst of a period of partic-

[3] *Ibid.* Emphasis added.
[4] *Ibid.*

ularly high tension, Finch agreed to meet with HEW employees who insisted that he fight for their views on major issues. These demands for a meeting came in the form of a petition signed by 2,000 employees requesting that the secretary meet with them on the agency's school desegregation policies following the resignation of HEW civil rights chief Leon Panetta.[5] However, as the time of the meeting drew closer, Finch and his advisors appeared to have second thoughts. At the last moment the secretary failed to appear because of illness, and the meeting was never held. The pulling and hauling between insistent HEW employees whom Finch seemed to want to satisfy and the more conservative White House view, which he as the president's protégé felt especially tied to, produced an untenable situation. Finch resigned in mid-1970, and was reassigned to the post of White House counselor.

Finch was succeeded as secretary of HEW by Elliot Richardson, at the time undersecretary of state. Richardson, too, had his difficult moments with the White House, but proved to be much more skillful and independent in his relationships with HEW bureaucrats. In fact, Richardson's success with the bureaucracy no doubt contributed to his transfer to the post of secretary of defense in 1973. He got along so well with the HEW's permanent staff, and there was such a high level of mutual respect between the secretary and the bureaucracy, that the White House power brokers became suspicious. Richardson's speeches praised HEW bureaucrats just at the time the White House was quietly readying a major offensive against them. On May 24, 1972, for example, at an awards ceremony for outstanding federal employees, Richardson challenged critics of career civil servants. He warned against "blaming bureaucrats for all the failings—real or imagined—of government. . . . To a degree that I feel is not unimportant, such mindless criticism can have a detrimental effect on the ability of the government to serve the public." If on this occasion Richardson's phrase, "mindless criticism," was noted in the White House, it was bound to have been resented. Richardson's transfer was also a reflection of his generally more liberal views on domestic issues at a time when the tone and emphasis of domestic policy was shifting to the right. Welfare reform was a major cause of tension between Richardson and the White House in 1972.

Nixon believed his family assistance plan was a balanced plan that involved both more generous benefits to some recipients and a strong work requirement for all able-bodied adults on welfare. Liberal Republicans in HEW tended to emphasize the first part and forget the second part of this equation. They highlighted increased benefits and played down the work requirement in the Nixon plan. Richardson worked closely with this liberal group. The reaction in the White House can be described as extreme irritation—irritation that Nixon's welfare reform plan was getting away from him. When the family as-

---

[5]Panetta is now a Democratic member of the U.S. House of Representatives.

sistance plan finally died in the Congress in 1972, one of the reasons for its demise was this conflict between the White House and HEW officials over its nature and purposes.[6]

In addition to preidentification and co-option pressures, there are strong outside forces that influence cabinet members to adopt an advocacy role for their agency. The most notable are from congressional committees and interest groups. These two groups often join with the bureaucracy in the triple alliances of function that develop around specific program interests of the federal government. John Gardner, as secretary of HEW, once referred to these functional power systems as "the not-so-holy Trinities." The customary political science term is "iron triangles." Cabinet members have to deal not only with strong program bureaucracies within the agency, but also with the other two legs of these iron triangles—congressional committees and interest groups. They court and cajole the cabinet officer in much the same fashion as does his own bureaucracy. These outside influences, moreover, are important to success; the secretary must go regularly to the Congress for funds, program authority, and the confirmation of key aides. Sometimes, too, he needs friends at public hearings where he could be embarrassed. Support from members of the Congress and friendly testimony from affected outside groups are valuable assets.

Political science professor David Truman had these kinds of conditions in mind in 1958 when he portrayed the cabinet member as in a position "where consciously or unconsciously he finds himself speaking primarily for the elements that had to be considered in his being selected and confirmed."[7] While Professor Truman acknowledged that the president can discipline cabinet members in extraordinary cases (for example, the firing of Nixon's first interior secretary, Walter Hickel), he contended that "a skillful department head who maintains strong support among the interest groups affected by his agency and among members of Congress can be virtually free to ignore the preferences of the Chief Executive."[8] Many presidents and presidential advisors have written about these pressures for conformity on cabinet secretaries. President Kennedy's principal aide for domestic issues, Theodore Sorensen, described cabinet officers as "bound by inherent limitations."

> . . . each department has its own clientele and point of view, its own experts and bureaucratic interests, its own relations with the Congress and certain subcommittees, its own statutory authority, objectives, and standards of success. No Cabinet member is free to ignore all this without impairing the morale and efficiency of his

[6]There were other reasons as well, having to do with flaws in the design of Nixon's family assistance plan that escalated its costs.

[7]David B. Truman, *The Governmental Process* (New York: Alfred A. Knopf, 1958), p. 407.

[8]*Ibid.*

department, his standing therein, and his relations with the powerful interest groups and Congressmen who consider it partly their own.[9]

THE CABINET ROLE IS DOWNGRADED

As experience was accumulated, Nixon's ideas on the relative roles of the White House staff and domestic cabinet officers underwent a fundamental shift. During the 1968 presidential transition, Nixon had stated that he did not intend to have the White House staff running domestic affairs the way Joseph Califano had during the Johnson administration. According to columnists Rowland Evans and Robert Novak:

> Not only was there not to be another Sherman Adams, there was to be no spiritual successor to Joseph Califano, President Johnson's top domestic aide of his latter years in power. Nixon lieutenants and Nixon himself had heard stories of Joe Califano, the tough young lawyer from Brooklyn by way of Harvard, harassing and riding herd on distinguished Cabinet members many years his senior. There would be no repetition of this in the Nixon administration where power would flow back to the Cabinet-level departments.[10]

The first clue of Nixon's change in attitude was in the handling of cabinet meetings. In the early days, there was frequent contact between the president and his domestic cabinet, both in small groups and in larger sessions. Meetings in forums such as the subcommittees of the Urban Affairs Council under staff director Moynihan were held regularly.

But this did not last long. It soon became apparent that such groups could not engage in candid discussions of major issues, especially if they were politically sensitive or involved large expenditures. Cabinet members invariably sought recognition at Urban Affairs Council meetings to plug their own often costly proposals, as yet unreviewed by the White House or the Budget Bureau. This put the president on the spot. He saw himself as in the position either of appearing to be unresponsive to major problems or of being drawn unwittingly into endorsing big new ventures without adequate study.

Cabinet-level meetings on domestic policy began to be held less frequently after the middle of 1969. Even when they were held, White House aides began to enter the picture more forcefully. They often scheduled noncontroversial subjects for discussion, highlighting dramatic but low-cost programs with

[9]Theodore C. Sorensen, *Decision-making in the White House: The Olive Branch or the Arrows* (New York: Columbia University Press, 1963), pp. 68–69.

[10]Rowland Evans, Jr., and Robert D. Novak, *Nixon in the White House: The Frustration of Power* (New York: Random House, 1971), p. 11.

strong publicity appeal. Later, the White House reacted by strengthening other decision systems—notably those of the White House staff—that would allow adequate program and fiscal review of major new proposals in the domestic sector.

THE WHITE HOUSE COUNTER-BUREAUCRACY EMERGES

The role of the White House staff began to change at the end of Nixon's first year in office. Contrary to Nixon's original plans, the staff was enlarged and its power expanded. By the end of Nixon's third year in office, the total executive office staff had doubled in cost from the Johnson years. The White House staff itself, along with borrowed agency personnel, occupied almost all of the space in the six floors of the Old Executive Office Building next to the White House. The Bureau of the Budget (renamed the Office of Management and Budget in July 1970) was displaced to new quarters across Pennsylvania Avenue. One account in 1972 noted ironically that President Nixon, "distrustful of

*"How about a bold move to reach dissenters—like if we were to
open direct talks with members of our Administration?"*

(From *Herblock's State of the Union*, Simon & Schuster, 1972.)

bureaucracy . . . has built a kind of defense against it—and in doing so he has built his own bureaucracy."[11]

Even more important than the increase in White House staff was the change in style. Under Ehrlichman, who became executive director of the new Domestic Council set up in 1970, the technique of the White House "working group" was adopted. The first working group was assigned to develop the president's welfare-reform program. Headed by one of Ehrlichman's lieutenants, Edward Morgan, Jr., this group included representatives from the Departments of Labor and HEW and the Bureau of the Budget. Less regular agency participants were from the Office of Economic Opportunity, the Department of Agriculture, and the Council of Economic Advisors.

The welfare working group met five to six hours a day every day over a period of ten weeks. Direct relationships were established between White House staff and agency officials well below the level of the secretary. Only the most astute cabinet member could keep on top of this policy process. The typical decision pattern was one of consensus building within the working group, with the lead and arbitrating role assigned to Ehrlichman or his deputy. If a member of a working group could not win his point by effective argument, he could go back and persuade his secretary to become personally involved. But by then, the cabinet officer had the difficult task of arguing an intricate policy position when most of the other participants were already knowledgeable about and committed to another policy. It was no wonder that cabinet members intervened less and less frequently during this period.

An example of how this process could be frustrating to cabinet secretaries occurred in the case of welfare. Several times, the welfare working group decided to pay cash instead of giving food stamps to needy persons eligible for family assistance benefits. Each time this decision surfaced in public, Agriculture Secretary Hardin angrily called the White House demanding to know why he had not been consulted. When it was explained to him that his representative, an assistant secretary, had been present in the working group, he complained that this was the wrong person and that he should have been told directly.

The final outcome of this food stamp question revealed something about White House operations during this period, particularly the role of Ehrlichman. The decision to "cash-out" (i.e., eliminate) food stamps for persons covered by the family assistance plan would have resulted in a politically unrealistically low level of total benefits for eligible families in many states. Just before the press briefing to unveil the new program, members of the working group tried to convince Ehrlichman to reconsider this position, contending that this decision could not possibly stick. Ehrlichman stood fast. He directed that if a

[11] *U.S. News and World Report*, April 24, 1972, p.72.

question about food stamps was asked, the answer should be given in no uncertain terms that families aided by the family assistance program would no longer be eligible to receive food stamps. The question was asked, the requisite answer was given, and the results were as predicted. Although the family assistance plan as a whole was well received when it was announced, there was strong criticism of the decision on food stamps. In less than ten days, it was reversed.

The White House relied on working groups increasingly in 1969 and 1970 as the president's domestic program was taking shape. Besides welfare, they covered emergency labor disputes, model cities, urban growth policy, health, revenue sharing, education, school desegregation, social services, and transportation. Many of these groups worked effectively, and it can be argued that their role in policy formulation across agency lines was an appropriate one. Nevertheless, the position of the cabinet officers and the structure of White House decision making were changing. In important ways they were becoming more like Lyndon Johnson's White House under Joseph Califano, a model that President Nixon at the outset had explicitly rejected.

John Ehrlichman explained the rationale for the working group approach in one of his few public statements on the subject, in November 1970. He argued that the White House should draw directly on the experts who know best the substance of matters under review.

> Now, some time ago, we sent out a request that we be furnished with the names of the people in the departments and agencies who actually did the work on the documents that come over. We found that everything was signed by the Secretary, and it didn't do much good to call the Secretary, and say: Say, about that paper you sent over here on so-and-so. As you know very well when somebody has a working knowledge of the document, we want those names because we want to be able to get those people over here to sit down with the President and answer his questions.[12]

On some occasions, the entire membership of a Domestic Council working group was brought in to meet with the president. Again, according to Ehrlichman,

> The young lawyers who worked on that came from different departments—Transportation, Labor, Bureau of the Budget, Council of Economic Advisors—people all over the government came in. There were ten young fellows—I don't think there was anybody in there over forty—in this session. They sat around the cabinet table on one side, the President on the other, and he just shot questions from those fel-

[12]Federal Executive Institute, U.S. Civil Service Commission, *The Challenges of Leadership for American Federal Executives*, Charlottesville, Va., November 1970.

lows for about forty-five minutes or an hour, drawing upon his experience during the Taft-Hartley episode when he was in Congress—trying alternatives with them, asking them questions about the work problem. And then he pulled off; he very seldom makes a decision in a meeting of that kind. Later, he asked for an additional presentation on one option that had been given to him.[13]

Steps were taken in this period to limit the use of the working group approach to issues that had what Ehrlichman called "multidimensional character," leaving to the individual cabinet secretary those "strictly within the scope of his authority."[14] But in the field of domestic policy, with its high degree of overlap among agency and program jurisdictions, opportunities for White House involvement even under this definition were multiple and far-ranging.

As the White House staff grew, new staff members became involved at lower levels in the agencies. Increasingly, Domestic Council staff took on an oversight role for existing programs and on routine legislative matters, as well as for many purely administrative decisions. White House clearance was required on more and more issues and became harder to obtain. On occasion, cabinet members were completely left out of White House deliberations. Then, their role in the inner councils of the administration was that of critics of planned new initiatives, defenders of the status quo. Access to the president became steadily more difficult to gain. Cabinet members often complained about the White House running their affairs.

The effects of this situation were predictable. When a junior White House staffer calls a career expert in an agency, that expert can develop his own line into the White House. This process further isolates the cabinet secretary and reinforces the tendency for the secretary and his close associates to draw up ranks and act on the basis of *we* versus *they*—*they* in this case being the president's staff. The bigger the White House establishment, the harder it is to keep this adversarial relationship from becoming dominant. As the counter-bureaucracy grew, the president's early concept of a strong, independent role for his cabinet officers increasingly was undermined, *and deliberately so.*[15]

The firing of Interior Secretary Walter Hickel in 1970 was in part a result of problems created by this system. When Hickel came to swords' point with

[13]*Ibid.* This quote from Ehrlichman concerns the development of legislation in the field of labor-management relations.

[14]*Ibid.*

[15]The White House staff in 1970 and 1971 was sensitive about these developments, and attempted in various ways to improve relationships with cabinet members. At one point a system was developed for staff members to submit standard forms with recommendations of instances in which the president could telephone cabinet members and congratulate them personally for particular actions they had taken. This arrangement never worked and was soon dropped.

President Nixon in the fall of 1970, he complained that the president was "isolated just sitting around listening to his staff."[16] Hickel said sometimes the White House would send him letters opposing proposals he had made and that the letters were signed by people he had never heard of. The Interior Department was not the only agency with such problems. HEW aides also complained in this period that the working group system was used to deal with issues exclusively in the province of HEW, as in the case of education and social service legislation. Finch's staff objected when the HEW personnel appointed to working groups were not of the secretary's choosing. This was the case, for example, when the conservative general counsel of HEW, Robert Mardian, who later resigned because of problems in his relationship with Finch, was named to the cabinet committee on school desegregation.

When George Romney in August 1972 announced his intention to leave the cabinet, he complained publicly about not even being able to get in to see the president. Other cabinet members were unhappy for the same reason. Even when they were successful in obtaining an appointment, they were often asked to submit a written agenda in advance and to provide assurance that they would not bring up subjects excluded from the agenda.

The very nature of Nixon's New Federalism program accentuated these problems. As pointed out in Chapter 2, a program designed to take power away from federal bureaucracies was bound to stir up the waters in Washington. Domestic cabinet members were caught in the middle. They were being cut out of decisions as the White House dug deeper into agency affairs, and at the same time they were being pressed very hard by their own program bureaucracies that were bent on preserving programs that had been designated for decentralization.

THE SELECTION OF SUBCABINET APPOINTEES

The change in the relationship between the White House and appointed officials involved not just the cabinet secretaries but also subcabinet officials (such as deputy and assistant secretaries and appointed agency heads) and advisors. The shift for the subcabinet was most clearly manifested by changes made in the appointment process.

Evans and Novak, in their book on the first two years of the Nixon administration, recount a crucial incident that reveals Nixon's view on subcabinet appointment in the earliest days. They report that at one of the first cabinet meet-

---

[16]*New York Times*, November 26, 1970. For a description of Hickel's experiences, see his account, *Who Owns America?* (Englewood Cliffs, N.J.: Prentice-Hall, 1971).

ings the president, in a mood they characterize as impulsive, delegated to cabinet officers the responsibility for filling all appointive positions in their agencies. He said they should choose on the basis of ability first and loyalty second. At the end of the meeting, the president is said to have turned to an aide and remarked, "I just made a big mistake."[17]

This initial decision to assign responsibility to cabinet members for the selection of the political appointees in their agency does not mean the White House completely lacked interest in who held the key posts. At the outset, White House domestic matters were largely in the hands of predominantly academic advisors, notably Moynihan and Arthur F. Burns, a counselor to the president. Nevertheless, some measure of political surveillance over political appointments was attempted. Although HEW Secretary Finch was able to appoint James Allen, a liberal New York State education commissioner, to HEW's top education post and other individuals with similar views to equally important positions, he could not pass muster with Boston health administrator John Knowles, whom the American Medical Association strongly opposed as assistant secretary for health.

In this period, White House surveillance of appointments to high-level domestic posts, to the extent exercised, was maintained by Chief of Staff H. R. Haldeman and by John Ehrlichman. A small review staff for political appointments was in operation. It was headed by Harry Flemming, son of Arthur Flemming, who had been secretary of HEW under President Eisenhower. Flemming reviewed appointments for political clearance and was responsible for making recommendations to fill commissions and specialized posts, but his executive search capability was limited, as was his influence over major agency positions.

All of this changed in the fall of 1970, when the White House counter-bureaucracy for domestic affairs was being established. In September 1970, the Flemming operation was replaced by a new group headed by Frederick Malek, a former deputy undersecretary of HEW, who reported directly to Haldeman. Malek's forte at HEW had been the removal and Siberian placement of HEW officials felt to be a problem for the administration, as well as the selection of management-oriented new appointees. His White House duties were no change of pace. Hereafter, the White House role in the selection and approval of key agency officials was much stronger.

Malek, on behalf of the president, undertook to review and clear all major political appointments, including staff assistants to top appointees, and also worked closely with cabinet officers to "identify" candidates for high posts. A soft-spoken, self-effacing person with strong political skills, he came to exert

[17]Evans and Novak, *op. cit.*, p. 70.

considerable influence in the president's inner circle, and in 1972 served as deputy director of the reelection campaign.[18]

ASSESSING THE WHITE HOUSE COUNTER-BUREAUCRACY APPROACH

By the end of President Nixon's first term, the strong-cabinet model had been fully displaced. The extent to which this had happened is best expressed, as truths often are, by satire. In May 1972, Russell Baker wrote a column in the *New York Times* on what he called Nixon's "secret cabinet." Commenting on John Connally's resignation as secretary of the treasury, Baker said everyone knows who Connally is, but who knows the other members of the cabinet? He said he had called the White House to inquire and was told that the list of cabinet members was not classified: "The White House simply didn't know who was in the cabinet." Baker claimed that by enterprising investigative reporting he was able to come up with answers and concluded his list of cabinet officers saying:

> The Secretary of Transportation is named Volpe, and the Secretary of Agriculture, Butz. Both were photographed with the President when they were appointed and are seen in Washington from time to time. Rumors that there is a Secretary of Labor are unfounded.[19]

The new White House control model had its problems and defects. The deeper the White House staff dug into agency affairs the more serious those problems became. By the middle of 1972, when the election intervened as the focus of attention of top administration officials, there was growing concern in the White House that the counter-bureaucracy technique was not the answer.

As the White House became more and more involved in routine administrative matters, the time and energy it could correspondingly devote to important policy issues was correspondingly reduced. This concern with routine matters acted like a mosquito bite; the more you scratched it, the more it itched. Senior White House staffers could not keep up with what their subordinates were doing. Moreover, the supply of talented aides for the White House who understood the substance and processes of domestic policy was limited. The

---

[18]Malek first came to public attention as a strong figure in the administration at the time of the Hickel firing when he informed Hickel's principal lieutenants that they too were terminated. Stories about his activities in this role, some surely apocryphal, were plentiful at HEW. He was said to have once visited an HEW field headquarters for what was expected to be a routine meeting on their operations and calmly informed all the top staff assembled to meet him that they were fired. Although probably not true in the way described, stories like this served to enhance Malek's effectiveness in the White House personnel position assigned to him in 1970.

[19]Russell Baker, *The New York Times*, May 23, 1972.

Republican Party's most able and experienced substantive experts preferred the more prestigious and visible agency posts. As the White House staff grew, its general caliber declined.

Robert Wood, a political scientist and secretary of housing and urban development in the Johnson administration, had written perceptively in 1969 about this dilemma under President Johnson.[20] Although his article on this subject was read in the White House, his advice was not heeded until considerable experience had proved the hard way that executive office control, no matter how well intended, is no way to run a government.

Wood described what he called "a curious inversion" of operations driving out policy as the executive office probes more deeply into program matters. His views are worth close attention:

> Confusion is created when men try to do too much at the top. In order to know what decisions are being made elsewhere in government, the White House tends either to spend time reviewing programs or to take more and more decisions on itself. The separate responsibilities of the White House, the Executive Office, and the agencies are fudged, and the demarcations of who does what become uncertain. The result is a blurring of the distinction between staff and line, between program and policy. Decisions tend to be reviewed and reviewed; and operational delays increase accordingly.

> As this confusion continues, a curious inversion occurs. Operational matters flow to the top—as central staffs become engrossed in subduing outlying bureaucracies—and policymaking emerges at the bottom. At the top, minor problems squeeze out major ones, and individuals lower down the echelons who have the time for reflection and mischief-making take up issues of fundamental philosophical and political significance.

Nixon's experience proved that Wood was right. Instead of weakening the position of the bureaucracy, the counter-bureaucracy tended to strengthen it. As Nixon's appointees in the White House and the executive agencies became more and more deeply involved in operational matters, lines of authority became blurred, decisions were delayed or never made, and career officials in the domestic program bureaucracies were in the catbird seat—just as Wood had predicted. Career bureaucrats found that when they went ahead and made important policy decisions on their own, no one knew that they did not have policy clearance. The responsible cabinet appointees were out of touch, too busy, or too harried by the White House to find out. Not only were domestic affairs not handled well under this type of system, but tensions arose as junior White House staffers second-guessed presidential appointees on matters that the lat-

[20]Robert Wood, "When Government Works," *The Public Interest*, Winter 1970.

ter thought were of relatively little consequence and that they should have been trusted to handle themselves or to delegate to others.

As his new term got underway in late 1972 and early 1973, the president himself complained that the White House staff has grown "like Topsy."[21] It was often impossible to find out who was handling a particular matter, much less to decide which one of several crosscutting decision systems in the White House should be assigned any given issue.

Within the bureaucracy itself, experienced hands knew how to take advantage of these conditions. The men and women who rise to the top in the federal service are themselves excellent politicians. They had seen all of this before. They could easily judge the level of program knowledge and experience of the different appointed officials. They could quickly figure out their relationships with one another. They could react skillfully when the klieg lights of presidential attention were focused on their programs; they could maneuver just as skillfully when they were not. In short, this was a system that did not work well for the president. It was against this background that the administrative presidency strategy was adopted as Richard Nixon's second term got underway.

[21]Statement at Camp David, November 27, 1972. See Document 4.

4

Nixon's Administrative Presidency Strategy

Richard Nixon's administrative presidency strategy, developed for his second term, had its roots in the work of the President's Advisory Council on Executive Organization. Like his predecessors, Nixon named a council on government organization almost immediately after his election in 1968. He chose as chairman his long-time associate and adviser, Roy Ash, then president of Litton Industries and later to become director of the Office of Management and Budget. Others on the six-man council were John Connally, former governor of Texas, who made a strong impression on the president for his work on the council; George Baker, dean of the Harvard Graduate School of Business; Frederick Kappel, former chairman of the board of the American Telephone and Telegraph Company; Walter Thayer, president of Whitney Communications; and Richard Paget, president of a consulting firm.

Like many of its predecessors, the Ash council straddled the key issue of the relative roles of the president's staff and cabinet officers. The initial phase of the council's work highlighted the role of the White House staff. Its first report recommended establishment of a Domestic Council in the White House (analogous to the National Security Council) and a reorganization of the Bureau of the Budget to highlight its management role.[1] Nixon formally an-

[1] The bureau under this plan was renamed the Office of Management and Budget. Originally, the Ash council had urged that the new name be simply Office of Management, but old-timers in the bureau and its director at the time, Robert Mayo, argued successfully that the word "budget" be retained in the new title.

nounced his decision to accept both of these measures in a message to Congress on March 12, 1971.[2] The president said that reform of the executive office was the place to begin in improving the management of the executive branch as a whole.

Just a little over one year after adopting the Ash proposals, Nixon, in his 1971 state of the union message,[3] unveiled an ambitious set of recommendations to reorganize the executive branch. Again, his proposals were based on the work of the Ash council. Nixon proposed regrouping seven of the existing cabinet agencies into four new superagencies—human resources, community development, natural resources, and economic affairs. In a special message to Congress, the president spelled out his reasons for advancing these reforms. The aim, he said, was to establish a system under which line control over the bureaucracy would be exercised by presidentially appointed program officials responsible for major goals of the administration.

> The responsibilities of each department would be defined in a way that minimizes parochialism and enables the President and the Congress to hold specific officials responsible for the achievement of specific goals.[4]

These arrangements were described as reflecting the president's management philosophy "that we should give clear assignments to able leaders—and then be sure that they are equipped to carry them out." Nixon said the new plan would help make the bureaucracy more accountable to elected leaders.

> No wonder the bureaucracy has sometimes been described as "the rule of no one." No wonder the public complains about programs which simply seem to drift. When elected officials cannot hold appointees accountable for the performance of government, then the voters' influence on government's behavior is also weakened.[5]

It seems ironic that while the president in March 1971 was publicly calling for a stronger role for his cabinet officers by endorsing the Ash council plan, the actual workings of his newly formed counter-bureaucracy in the White House were weakening the role of the cabinet secretary. Nevertheless, it is possible to reconcile these two developments.

Toward the end of Richard Nixon's first year in office, he apparently concluded that because of the weaknesses of existing management structures he

---

[2]It was not surprising that Nixon accepted the Ash council plans; the group had met with him and his top staff at long meetings several times before completing its work on the executive office.

[3]See Document 2.

[4]Presidential Message on Executive Reorganization, March 25, 1971. See Document 3.

[5]*Ibid.*

needed to create a stronger means of exercising authority over major govern-ment agencies in order to achieve his policy aims. At the same time, he ap-peared to have decided that many of the men he had named to head the biggest-spending domestic agencies and their principal lieutenants were not able, or disposed, to carry out his policies. They held points of view very different from his. The traditional strategy of a balanced cabinet of distinguished men and women of independent national reputation was preventing Nixon from pursu-ing his policy goals.

It was in this setting that Nixon first acted in 1970 to develop his counter-bureaucracy system to grab the reins more firmly. But, as already observed, this approach did not work well. Even a significantly enlarged White House and executive office staff was no match for the far larger numbers of agency personnel. Members of the new counter-bureaucracy could not get a handle on all of the programs and activities of government that had a bearing on Nixon's policy objectives. They could not even come close to doing so. They could not keep track of each other, much less the operations of a large number of major government agencies. The caliber of the White House staff assigned to sub-stantive matters was not up to the challenge. It became increasingly clear to Nixon and his principal aides that over the long run, other and more perma-nent controls over the bureaucracy would be needed.

Thus the president and his chief aides ultimately came to regard the new White House counter-bureaucracy as, at best, a temporary and partial tech-nique to be succeeded by more sweeping changes to establish a deeper and more durable system of agency-based controls. That is what the second Ash council report appeared to offer, and for this reason Nixon proposed the new superagencies, which would allow a relatively small number of Nixon's top ap-pointees to exercise effective policy and management control. These legislative proposals, however, fared badly on Capitol Hill. Therefore, Nixon attempted to implement the philosophy and aims of the Ash council reorganization plan as much as possible *without legislation*. The president would place his own trusted appointees in positions to directly manage key elements of the bureauc-racy without elaborate White House or executive office staff machinery. The new appointees would be the president's men. They would have clear lines of authority. The bureaucracy would report to them; they would be held account-able.

The basic point for purposes of this analysis is that Nixon came to the con-clusion sometime in 1971 that in many areas of government, particularly do-mestic affairs, *operations is policy*. Many day-to-day management tasks for domestic programs—for example, regulation writing, grant approval, and budget apportionment—are substantive and therefore involve policy. The White House counter-bureaucracy could not penetrate deeply enough into the operations of government on any kind of systematic basis to effect these essen-

Richard Hood and his Merry Men

(Courtesy Draper Hill. Copyright *The Commercial Appeal*, Memphis, Tenn.)

tially managerial processes. Gaining greater control over agency policy setting and managerial processes was the aim of Nixon's administrative presidency strategy in his second term.

1972 ELECTION TRIGGERS CHANGE

It is apparent in retrospect that Nixon had decided to move emphatically on this management strategy well before his reelection. He acted with what can only be called lightning swiftness once the election had been held.

The day after the election, press secretary Ronald Ziegler announced that the president had retired at 2:30 A.M. but was back at his desk the next day at 8 A.M. and had immediately begun working on reorganization plans for the new term. Nixon held a cabinet meeting that same day and, after thanking his associates for their help in the campaign, proceeded to outline dramatic plans for staff changes. He required that all political appointees submit their resignations forthwith. While requests of this kind have been made before, they were usually on a *pro forma* basis. Here the stated objective was to accept many resignations and use this process as an opportunity for what Ziegler referred to as a "shake-up."[6] Each cabinet officer was instructed to meet with the principal appointed officials of his agency and request letters of resignation with the understanding that many would be accepted.[7] Tension at departmental conference tables ran high at a time when in the normal course of events one would have expected instead a mood of celebration and relaxation. Pundits in Washington had a field day. One comment was set to the tune of "Three Blind Mice":

> Richard Nixon's changing the guard.
> The Cabinet's taking it terribly hard
> Will we be hoist on our own petard
> For four more years?[8]

Having set this house-cleaning process in motion, the president departed for Key Biscayne, Florida, on Thursday, November 9. When he returned to

[6]UPI, November 8, 1972.

[7]It is perhaps indicative of the style of Nixon's White House staff that they chose this heavy-handed tactic when other approaches appeared to be available. For example, a more discreet announcement could have been made that officials not planning to stay at least another two years in subcabinet positions should so indicate. Then, in every case where a resignation was to be "accepted," a face-saving announcement could have been made by the agency or the White House that the "firee" had indicted his or her wishes to move back into private life before the end of 1976.

[8]Joseph Young, "Four More Years, Lament of an Ousted Aide," "Nixon Looks Ahead," *Washington Star-News*, January 23, 1973.

"I didn't realize it applied just to him."

(From *Herblock Special Report*, W. W. Norton & Co. Inc., 1974.)

Washington the following week, he moved his working headquarters to Camp David in Maryland's Catoctin Mountains. There, he met with top White House aides and conducted individual meetings with cabinet members and persons in the running for major posts. He chose Camp David, Ziegler said, because "He likes to work up there. . . . He doesn't have the pressures he does in the White House for outside appointments."[9]

Rumors and leaks were widespread in this period. The uncertainty that this process produced brought government decision processes to a virtual halt. The president's daily schedule was reported by Ziegler with hints of what was to come. But the clearest signals in this period emanated from the president himself in an interview he gave to *Washington Star-News* reporter Garnett D. Horner on the Sunday before the election for use afterward.[10] The Horner interview appeared November 9 and was widely quoted.

Nixon, in this interview, concentrated on domestic programs. He said he

[9]UPI, November 11, 1972.
[10]See Document 5.

would "shuck off" and "trim down" social programs that in his view reflected the failures of the 1960s.[11] He talked specifically about cutting governmental employment: "I honestly believe that government in Washington is too big and is too expensive. . . . We can do the job better with fewer people."[12] He referred to some agencies as "too fat, too bloated," and made it clear, according to Horner, that he was talking about domestic agencies, such as the Department of Housing and Urban Development (HUD), the Department of Health, Education, and Welfare (HEW), and the Department of Transportation.[13]

As the reshuffling process got under way in earnest, the president through Ziegler set a target of December 15 for completing the new cabinet. Announcements of its members commenced on November 28, 1972, the day after Nixon made a public statement in the helicopter hangar at Camp David about his plans for the second term.[14] The president, in this statement, noted that second terms in history tend to run downhill and lack vitality and that through his various new appointments and reorganization measures he was trying to "change the historical pattern." Nixon's statement included a hint about Caspar Weinberger, then director of the Office of Management and Budget, whom he described as an example of an official he had prevailed on to accept another position. He also said that two men, previously reported to be high in the rankings, would not be in the new cabinet by their own choosing—Governor Nelson Rockefeller of New York and the former Texas governor and treasury secretary, John Connally.

In his November 27 statement, the president also zeroed in on the growth of the White House counter-bureaucracy. "It is now time to reverse that growth by bringing Cabinet members into closer contact with the White House and, of course, the President himself."[15] Later, in his 1974 budget, the president carried out the commitment made in this period to cut in half the number of executive office personnel. He proposed a reduction from 4,250 employees in the 1973 budget to 1,686 in 1974. (Eighty percent of this reduction, however, was accounted for by the elimination of the Office of Economic Opportunity.)

Nixon's various statements in 1972 about the need for strong cabinet officers and the simultaneous cuts in the White House staff reflected his willingness now to *make a choice*. He would opt for strong cabinet officers as opposed to a White House-based control system for domestic affairs. It is interesting that, in the midst of the Watergate period, Nixon decided to make a deliberate attempt to reduce the power and importance of the White House staff. There

[11]Garnett D. Horner, *Washington Star-News*, November 9, 1972.
[12]*Ibid.*
[13]*Ibid.*
[14]See Document 4.
[15]Horner, *op. cit.*

may have been a connection in the president's mind (either conscious or unconscious) between Watergate and the administrative presidency. However, there was no clue at the time that this was so. To the contrary, it was Haldeman and Ehrlichman who emerged at the top of the new structure.

Ehrlichman survived this process because it was his Domestic Council staff system that was being replaced. Part of the reason he survived was that Ehrlichman was among the key persons, along with Haldeman, Ash, and Malek (deputy director of OMB), who diagnosed the weaknesses of the counter-bureaucracy approach. Another reason for Ehrlichman's longevity under Nixon was the chemistry of his relationship with Nixon. A president, or any other executive for that matter, can work closely with only a few trusted subordinates. Every presidency is heavily influenced by the personality and style of the people closest to the president. Nixon's presidency was fatally affected by his choices. In contrast, Reagan's presidency (as Chapters 5 and 6 demonstrate) has benefited from the longer perspective and more even-handed and less excitable temperament of the people closest to Reagan.

NEW CABINET ANNOUNCED

On November 28, 1972, exactly twenty-one days after the election, the announcements of Nixon's new cabinet officers for the second term began. Not surprisingly the first was that Weinberger would be nominated as secretary of HEW and that the much more liberal incumbent, Elliot Richardson, would be moving to the Department of Defense.[16] Weinberger was to be succeeded at OMB by Roy Ash. Richardson, in turn, replaced Melvin Laird, who on several occasions had indicated his intention to return to private life at the end of the first term. The Weinberger-Richardson switch was particularly interesting. Both would now be in positions where it would be to their and the president's political advantage to hold down rather than build up federal programs. In Richardson's case, however, his number-two man was a counterbalancing conservative, William Clements, a Texas oil company executive.[17]

On the day after the Weinberger-Richardson-Ash announcements, Nixon named a new secretary of labor, Peter Brennan, a "hard hat" and president of the New York City Building and Construction Trades Council. He was to replace incumbent James Hodgson, who it was said had been asked to consider another high-level post in the international area and was also weighing a return

---

[16]Weinberger at OMB was noted as a man who kept his cards close to his vest. Apparently he behaved the same way at HEW. In an article in the *Washington Star* (March 29, 1973), headlined appropriately, "This Caspar is No Milquetoast," Judith Randall referred to him as follows: "In short, the man is simply a master of obfuscation, not to be matched or even copied by mere journeyman obfuscators like senators and representatives."

[17]Clements is currently governor of Texas.

to private life. Brennan proved to be an unhappy choice as a replacement for Hodgson who, though he lacked color, had presided over an able staff that had performed effectively in many areas.

After Brennan, the announcements came rapidly. Three cabinet officers were to remain in their posts—George Shultz at Treasury, Earl Butz at Agriculture, and William Rogers at State. Shultz was also elevated to a new post as assistant to the president for economic affairs. The intention was to create a central staff mechanism under Shultz that would coordinate economic policy decisions in the manner envisioned by the president's March 1971 proposal for a new superagency for economic affairs.

The new strategy also moved many second-level White House aides to key management posts. A number of loyal subcabinet officials were promoted and several members of Ehrlichman's Domestic Council staff were assigned to critical line positions in domestic agencies. In every case, these appointees fit the pattern of trusted associates who were not luminaries in their own right. Among the subcabinet officials elevated in this period, Undersecretary of Commerce James Lynn, a little-known but highly respected Nixon stalwart, received the top designation. Lynn was named secretary of housing and urban development; Romney's departure plans had already been announced. On the other hand, Lynn's boss at the time, Secretary of Commerce Peter Peterson, an increasingly prominent figure in this usually lesser post, was removed. This was undoubtedly a reflection of Peterson's tendency toward strong argument within the inner councils of the administration and of high visibility outside. Peterson was quoted bitterly as saying he had failed his physical for reappointment: "His calves were too thick and he could not click his heels."[18]

THE SUPERSECRETARIES

Nixon's administrative strategy for his second term went beyond shifts in the persons named to top posts. As part of the new plan, the president put into effect another key element of his March 1971 reorganization proposals—the regrouping of domestic governmental responsibilities among cabinet agency heads.

This aspect of Nixon's administrative presidency strategy was unveiled two weeks before the inauguration. On January 5, 1973, Nixon announced that certain cabinet officers would be given special roles as "counselors to the presi-

---

[18] *Washington Post*, December 26, 1972. Another example of an agency in which important changes were made in second-level administrators was HEW. For a study of how these changes were tied to shifts in welfare policy, see Ronald Randall, "Presidential Power versus Bureaucratic Intransigence: The Influence of the Nixon Administration on Welfare Policy," *American Political Science Review*, vol. 73, no. 3, September 1979, pp. 795–810.

dent'' in addition to heading their own agencies. The new designations closely followed the Ash council recommendations. The three supersecretaries, who were also appointed to chair Domestic Council committees for their respective areas, were Secretary of Agriculture Butz for natural resources; Secretary of HEW Weinberger for human resources; and Secretary of HUD Lynn for community development. This was in addition to the designation already made of Shultz as an assistant to the president in economic affairs.

Paralleling the changes in the cabinet, four men were selected by the president as his principal White House assistants ''to integrate and unify policies and operations throughout the executive branch . . . and to oversee the activities for which the president is responsible.'' They were Haldeman, Ehrlichman, Roy Ash, and Secretary of State Henry Kissinger.[19] In conjunction with these White House changes, the president pledged that the total personnel complement of the executive office would be cut in half. The lesson of Robert Wood's ''curious inversion'' had been learned, albeit the hard way. The new supersecretaries would have plenty of room to operate in their assigned spheres of activity. They would also have opportunity on a regular basis for direct contact with the president.

An examination of the roles assigned the supersecretaries shows the new relationships that were anticipated among cabinet members. Some were to be more equal than others. The supersecretaries were in a position to pass on policy decisions and program matters that had formerly been the responsibility of other cabinet officers. For example, manpower programs (in the Labor Department) were assigned to Secretary of HEW Weinberger. Public transit programs of the Department of Transportation were assigned to James Lynn as supersecretary for community development. Many natural resource activities in the Interior Department were to be under Earl Butz as the high commissioner for natural resources.[20] Taken together, Nixon's approach for running

[19]In the first term, the management strategy in the domestic area had been based on Kissinger's experience in foreign policy. The Domestic Council staff under Ehrlichman was in many ways modeled after Kissinger's effective approach to running the National Security Council. In the second term, the tables were turned. The administrative presidency strategy undoubtedly was a major reason that the president moved Kissinger to the State Department as secretary.

[20]Secretary of the Interior Rogers C. B. Morton was disappointed by Butz's designation as supersecretary for natural resources. Although a long-time associate of Nixon's and a former Republican national chairman, Morton apparently was not as highly regarded by the White House inner circle. Butz had made a strong impression as a Nixon stalwart when he succeeded Clifford Hardin in 1972. Morton experienced a similar fate in 1973 when he was passed over as energy czar, a post he was said to have wanted. Despite these disappointments, he stayed on at Interior through both episodes and managed to still most of the comments about his personal feelings in these matters. When the Ford administration came into office his fortunes changed, since he had been a friend and colleague of the new president for many years when they both were members of the House of Representatives.

the government in his second term, based on experience in the first term, had decisively changed.

The Watergate transcripts show the president's increasing concern about controlling the bureaucracy in his second term. At an April 19 meeting with Ehrlichman, Nixon complained bitterly, "We have no discipline in this bureaucracy." He added, "We never fire anybody. We never reprimand anybody. We never demote anybody. We always promote the sons-of-bitches that kick us in the ass."[21] The president in this instance demanded the firing of the director of the San Francisco regional office of the Small Business Administration. Nixon said he should be disciplined publicly, "as a warning to a few other people around in this government, that we are going to quit being a bunch of God-damn soft-headed managers."[22]

THE MEANING OF MANDATE

The administrative presidency strategy implemented in Nixon's second term represented not only a 180-degree shift in management tactics, but also a significant philosophical shift. The tone of the second term and the administration's policy positions involved a decided turn to the right, as Nixon took a more pessimistic and conservative position on domestic issues. In his first inaugural address, Nixon had emphasized the need to solve domestic problems; in his second inaugural address he stated: "I offer no solutions, no promise of a purely governmental solution for every problem. We have lived too long with that false hope."

The essential framework of the New Federalism was still in place, but the rhetoric was much sharper. Programs to be decentralized were criticized in much stronger language than previously. Those to be folded into block grants were described in the fiscal year 1974 budget as "failures," as "not having sufficient impact to justify continued funding" and as "not producing results commensurate with the costs." By contrast, the tone of the first term had been much more positive. The emphasis then had been on "reforms," with administration spokesmen often contending that federal grant-in-aid programs to be decentralized had served a good purpose and now could be assigned to state and local governments.

The meaning of mandate for domestic affairs in 1973 was expressed, not in the state of the union message as is customary, but in Nixon's tight-fisted budget message for fiscal year 1974, sent to the Congress January 29, 1973. The 1974 budget was especially hard-hitting on domestic programs. Even

---

[21]Transcript published in the *Washington Star-News*, July 20, 1974.
[22]The offending SBA official was never fired, although he was demoted.

though human resource programs had grown dramatically during his tenure,[23] Nixon now chose to play up their problems.

> . . . [D]isappointments and failures have accompanied these accomplishments. The seeds of those failures were sown in the 1960's when the "do something, do anything" pressure for Federal panaceas led to the establishment of scores of well-intentioned social programs too often poorly conceived and hastily put together.[24]

The 1974 budget message criticized throwing money at problems, a familiar refrain in this period. Said the president, "with vaguely defined objectives, incomplete plans of operation, and no effective means of evaluation, most of these programs simply did not do the job."

In the urban area, Nixon's 1974 budget was even more strident. All housing programs were suspended pending a review. Likewise, most programs for urban development were suspended with the stipulation that expenditures in these areas would begin again in the following fiscal year under urban special revenue sharing, now to be called the "Better Communities Act."[25]

Both in the human resource and community development areas, the budget for fiscal year 1974 proposed significant cuts. These reductions were to be accomplished through both legislative and administrative actions—by requesting appropriations well below the previous year's levels and by executing a series of budget impoundments. Impoundments were viewed as a way to use presidential authority to cut program levels and, in some instances, eliminate whole programs. This approach was unprecedented. In the past, the impoundment authority had been used primarily to delay funding for particular capital projects where previously approved plans could not be carried out on schedule.

At the end of the budget message, as is customary, there were the rhetorical flourishes that the president uses to state his main themes and directions. The 1974 Nixon budget message focused on the bureaucracy.

> Common sense tells us that it is more important to save tax dollars than to save bureaucratic reputations. By abandoning programs that have failed, we do not close our eyes to problems that exist; we shift resources to more productive uses.

It was the budget message and not the state of the union message that received most attention at the start of the second term. Nixon in 1973 was the

---

[23]See Table 2-1.

[24]Executive Office of the President, Office of Management and Budget, *Budget of the United States Government* (Washington, D.C.: U.S. Government Printing Office, 1973), p. 16.

[25]To some critics, the new plan was referred to, instead, as the Bitter Communities Act. A version of this bill closely resembling that proposed by Nixon was enacted in 1974. It was signed into law by President Ford.

first president since Woodrow Wilson who did not deliver his state of the union message to the Congress in person. Instead, it was broken down into a series of six program statements, each presented in the form of a short radio address. In domestic areas, Nixon's state of the union package for 1973 included four statements—on the environment, human resources, law enforcement, and community development. The last of these areas is the most interesting. In it, Nixon declared that the crisis of the cities had ended. Citing improved conditions on crime, air pollution, housing, urban violence, and city finances, the president said the "hour of crisis has passed." In addition to his strong criticism of the failures of human service programs and his paring down of environmental initiatives for budget reasons, the president's decision to end the war on urban decay and bring the troops home was the extreme point of the short-lived shift to the right in 1973.

As Watergate pressures mounted in 1973 and 1974 and the threat of impeachment loomed, the administration's domestic program shifted again. The state of the union and budget messages submitted in 1974 reflected a decided change of tune. With a tottering presidency facing an opposition Congress, the new strategy was to placate potential liberal opponents. The 1974 state of the union message had a much more positive tone. The new budget for fiscal year 1975 was conciliatory. Many of the proposed budget cuts of the previous year (i.e., those that the Congress in many cases had rejected) were not put forward again.

ALL FOR NAUGHT

Nixon's administrative initiatives of the second term—personnel shifts, budget impoundments, reorganization of the executive office, and decentralizing authority—were all for naught. On April 30, 1973, John Ehrlichman, the driving force behind the changes in domestic affairs, resigned because of Watergate. Soon the designations of the supersecretaries were officially removed. As the new White House staff was assembled in the late spring and summer of 1973, it came into being in a far different setting. The momentum of Nixon's lopsided 1972 election victory was dissipated. Decisive action, including unneeded fights with program bureaucracies and congressional committees, could not be undertaken now. Alexander Haig, Jr., Haldeman's successor, called for "an open presidency" with activist, independent roles for cabinet officers. The wheel had turned a full revolution.

White House control over the domestic agencies in the final days of the Nixon presidency was all but nonexistent. During his short tenure as Ehrlichman's successor, Melvin Laird showed no interest in the administrative presidency strategy. When he left, Kenneth Cole, Ehrlichman's former deputy, succeeded Laird. An able and experienced man with good judgment and an equally good personality, Cole apparently found little opportunity for management controls on the scale or on the basis previously planned. He made further cuts in the staff of the Domestic Council and kept a low profile. The Office of Management and Budget played a very strong role in this period, with the president and his top White House aides increasingly preoccupied by Watergate and attendant problems. But the predominant pattern was one of policy and administrative matters receding in importance as far as the White House was concerned. If they were considered at all, it was almost entirely in relation to political efforts to stave off impeachment.

A close aide to John Mitchell in the first term, Donald Santarelli, named at the start of the second term as director of the Law Enforcement Assistance Administration in the Justice Department, was one of the few brave souls to speak in what he thought was a private moment about these new conditions. He said he was his own boss now and didn't check with anyone about his decisions. "There is no White House anymore." Santarelli was forced to resign because of the wide press coverage of his remarks, but many others who saw things the same way and behaved accordingly (although without saying so) stayed on.

CHAPTER 5

Reagan's Domestic Agenda

In sharp contrast to the Nixon period, Reagan's domestic program has been executed through *a dual approach* that involves *both* legislative and administrative actions from the outset of his administration. This simultaneous pursuit of legislative and administrative aims is distinctive for the modern presidency. The Reagan administration's policy agenda for domestic affairs is discussed in this chapter; the administrative tactics are discussed in Chapter 6.

THE LIMITS OF GOVERNMENT

The substance of the Reagan presidency in domestic affairs is best understood by looking first at the way in which issues have been conceptualized. Instead of the past emphasis on *problems*, the Reagan administration has focused on *limitations*—limitations of the role of government, limitations in its ability to carry out its purposes, and limitations in its resources.

Three themes of Reagan's domestic policy stand out:

- One, a commitment to the idea that the public sector should be smaller and less intrusive, and that the private sector should be strengthened and made more influential.
- Two, a theory of federalism that involves reducing the role of the federal government by devolving national responsibilities to state governments.

(Courtesy Tony Auth. Copyright *The Philadelphia Inquirer*.)

Three, a concept of programs to aid the poor that consists of providing adequate benefits to the "truly needy," and removing from welfare able-bodied persons who can make it on their own.[1]

RECONCILIATION PROCESS

In keeping with the goal of a smaller federal government, Reagan forged his domestic program primarily through the budget process. When Reagan came to office in January 1982, the budget for federal fiscal year 1982 (October 1, 1981, through September 30, 1982) already had been transmitted to the Congress by Jimmy Carter. Within three months, the Reagan administration had proposed sweeping revisions of the federal budget. Reductions were proposed in more than 200 programs, with cuts of $180 billion proposed over a four-year period. Many of these cuts could only be achieved through changes in the basic authorizing legislation. (This was especially true for entitlement programs like food stamps, medicaid, and aid to families with dependent children.)

To enact such fundamental legislative initiatives, the administration employed a new legislative technique. Changes to the various laws were enacted in

[1]These ideas and themes are expressed in Reagan's inaugural address. See Document 8.

one piece of legislation, the Omnibus Reconciliation Act of 1981. A little-known provision of the Congressional Budget and Impoundment Control Act of 1974 provides for a "reconciliation" process. The Reagan administration carried the reconciliation process further than anything envisioned by the framers of the act.

Under OMB Director David Stockman's leadership, the Reagan administration proposed legislation in both the Senate and the House requiring nearly all committees of the Congress to take action to cut spending. Both authorizing and appropriations committees were required to make policy changes and spending cuts. These cuts and changes were made in response to "instructions" contained in the first budget resolution for fiscal year 1982. The committee recommendations were compiled into a single bill, the Omnibus Reconciliation Bill, which was adopted in a single "up-or-down" vote in both chambers. Members could either support the president or oppose him. When the dust settled, far-reaching substantive changes had been made in the domestic policies of the national government.

Table 5-1 shows how this reordering of priorities, which began under Carter in 1978, accelerated significantly under Reagan. At the top of the table we see that in two categories—grants to states and localities for other than welfare purposes and direct federal operations—spending was projected to decline under Reagan. The second section of the table shows that, when adjusted for inflation, total outlays from 1970 through 1978 rose by 4.1 percent per year. Under Carter this rate was basically unchanged. Under Reagan the rate of increase fell to 2.3 percent in fiscal year 1982.

REAGAN'S NEW FEDERALISM

White House officials maintain that President Reagan never used the term "New Federalism" for his domestic program, and that it originated with the press. They acknowledge that some administration officials (and even administration documents) have used the term, but that the president prefers to talk instead about the administration's "federalism initiatives." A possible reason for Reagan's reluctance to take up this term is the fact that Nixon used it. There are interesting differences between the two New Federalisms—Nixon's and Reagan's.

Both Reagan and Nixon embraced the idea of devolution, the transfer of responsibility and power from the central government to subnational governments.[2] The main difference is that Reagan proposed devolution from the na-

---

[2]The word "decentralization," which Nixon used, tends to be given a more restrictive meaning, referring to the transfer of administrative functions from the central government to states and localities.

Table 5-1   Growth Rates of Federal Outlays During the Carter Years

Type of Spending	FY 1971– FY 1978	FY 1978– FY 1981	FY 1981– FY 1982 (estimate)
Annual Percentage Growth in Current Dollars			
National defense	4.9	15.0	17.4
Payments to individuals	14.9	15.4	11.0
Direct payments	(15.2)	(15.4)	(12.1)
Grant payments	(13.5)	(15.5)	(3.9)
Other state and local grants	17.5	1.9	− 9.3
Net interest	13.4	24.8	20.8
All other operations	12.6	5.7	− 6.5
Total outlays	11.5	13.6	10.4
Annual Percentage Growth in 1972 Constant Dollars			
National defense	− 2.5	4.1	7.8
Payments to individuals	7.9	5.7	3.1
Direct payments	(8.2)	(5.7)	(4.0)
Grant payments	(6.7)	(5.6)	(− 3.4)
Other state and local grants	9.3	− 6.1	− 16.6
Net interest	6.3	14.6	11.5
All other operations	4.1	− 3.2	− 11.2
Total outlays	4.1	4.0	2.3

Source: Average annual percentage growth rates calculated from outlay data contained in Office of Management and Budget, *Federal Government Finances: 1983 Budget Data* (Washington, D.C., February 1982), tables 10 and 11, pp. 59–70. Growth rate from fiscal year 1981 to fiscal year 1982 is based on the February 1982 OMB estimate of fiscal year 1982 outlays.

tional government exclusively to the *states*—not to localities. Nixon, on the other hand, was more pragmatic. This is understandable. He faced a Congress in which both bodies were controlled by Democrats, whereas the Republican capture of a majority in the Senate in 1980 gave Reagan a great strategic advantage. Even if he had wanted to, Nixon probably would have been unable to obtain congressional approval of revenue sharing and block grants that involved only state governments. Under Nixon's revenue sharing and block grant programs, local governments (cities, counties, towns) received about three-fourths of the funds distributed.

A second major difference between the Reagan and Nixon brands of the New Federalism, again reflecting differences in the political setting, has to do with money. Nixon block grant proposals involved extra funds, called "sweeteners." The community development block grant (CDBG) program, for example, called for spending increases of 15 percent per year when enacted in 1974. The other major block grant enacted under Nixon, the Comprehensive Employment and Training Act (CETA), also contained a "sweetener." In contrast, the Reagan block grant proposals involved only bitter pills in the form of budget cuts. The cuts were justified on efficiency grounds. The result of creating new block grants, it was argued, was that overhead costs could be reduced and therefore funding for the categorical grants "folded in" to the new block grants could be appreciably lowered without impairing programs or services.

Although Reagan proposed consolidating eighty-five existing categorical grant programs into seven new block grants, Congress gave him only part of what he asked for. The reconciliation act passed in 1981 created nine "block grants" that affected fifty-four existing programs with total budget authority for fiscal year 1982 of $7.2 billion (see Table 5-2). Besides the lower dollar amounts, the result was more modest than what Reagan had asked for in other ways. Four of Reagan's "block grants" contained only one previously categorical program. Two of the programs were simply modified versions of existing block grants. Responsibility under all nine of Reagan's block grants enacted in 1981 was assigned to the states. Therefore, although the block grant program was less extensive than originally proposed, Reagan was able to achieve one of the major objectives of the New Federalism by devolving responsibility to the states.

SOCIAL SECURITY

The domestic issue that most bedeviled the Reagan administration in its first year was social security. Reagan suffered his most lopsided defeat in the Congress in 1981 on this issue. By a vote of 96–0, the Senate on May 19, 1981, re-

Table 5-2   New or Changed Block Grants in the 1981 Reconciliation Act

Grant	Number of Programs Consolidated	Final FY 1982 Budget Authority (millions of dollars)
Social services	3	2,400
Home energy assistance	1	1,875
Small city community development	1	1,037
Elementary and secondary education	29	470
Alcohol, drug abuse, and mental health	3	432
Maternal and child health	7	348
Community services	1	348
Primary health care	1	248
Preventive health and health services	8	82
Total for nine block grants	54	7,240

Source: John W.Ellwood, ed., *Reductions in U.S. Domestic Spending: How they Affect State and Local Governments* (New Brunswick, N.J.: Transaction Books, 1982), p. 341.

jected proposals for restructuring the social security system advanced by Richard Schweiker, secretary of health and human services. Opposition to the reform package was led by a coalition called "Save Our Security" (SOS), comprising one hundred groups including the AFL-CIO, the American Association of Retired Persons, and the National Retired Teachers Association. They denounced the plan as "a calamity, a tragedy, and a catastrophe."[3] Seeking to minimize the political damage caused by the Senate action, the administration immediately backpedaled. In a letter to congressional leaders on social security, the president acknowledged that "members of Congress on both sides of the aisle have alternative answers."[4] He said, "This diversity is healthy." The president asked Schweiker to meet with congressional leaders "to launch a bipartisan effort to save Social Security."[5]

The Schweiker plan was intended to ensure the short-term solvency of the social security system. It was expected to save $9 billion in fiscal year 1982, with total savings of $46.4 billion projected for the five-year period ending in 1987. The administration hoped that these savings would not only restore the financial integrity of the social security system, but would allow future reductions in the social security tax.

The administration's package consisted of eight proposals, of which six were designed to save money; the other two were included to make the package politically more palatable. By far the most controversial proposal concerned early retirement. Workers who retired at age sixty-two in 1981 received 80 percent of the benefits that they would have been entitled to receive if they had waited until age sixty-five to retire. The reform package proposed that, beginning in January 1982, early retirees receive 55 percent of their total benefits.

Of the five remaining cost-saving proposals, two were designed to reduce what was felt to be the overindexing of the social security system. Benefits are increased each year to match the increase in the cost of living, as measured by the consumer price index. The Schweiker plan proposed delaying the July 1982 increase until October 1982, and revising the computation formula to reduce benefits to future retirees. Other proposals would have substantially tightened up the availability and amounts of benefits.[6]

[3]Warren Weaver, Jr., "President Proposed Negotiating a Plan on Social Security," *New York Times*, May 22, 1981, p. 1.

[4]*Ibid.*

[5]*Ibid.*

[6]Two proposals that involved added cost were included to balance out this package. Individuals who continued to work after age sixty-five were to be allowed to retain progressively higher amounts of earnings. In 1981 benefits were reduced by one dollar for every two dollars earned in excess of $5,500 per year. The administration proposed that this ceiling be raised to $10,000 in 1983 and $15,000 in 1985, with no limit thereafter. The administration plan also recommended that the social security tax be lowered when the money in the trust fund reached 50 percent of the amount needed to fund the benefits required for the following year.

(By Jack Ohman. Reprinted by permission of Tribune Company Syndicate, Inc.)

In response to the 1981 defeat on social security, the president followed an age-old strategem. He appointed a commission to study the short-term and long-term needs of the social security system. The commission was explicitly charged to report in 1983—*after* the 1982 congressional elections.

WELFARE

President Reagan also took on his third major goal, reducing welfare spending, through the budget process. Many conservatives argue, as does Martin Anderson, Reagan's first domestic policy advisor in the White House, that under these programs there is "a 'poverty wall' that destroys the financial incentive to work for millions of Americans."[7] According to Anderson, "Free from basic wants, but heavily dependent on the State, with little hope of breaking free, they are a new caste, the 'Dependent Americans.'"[8]

The biggest impact by far of the Reagan budget cuts for fiscal year 1982 was on the poor. Among the poor, the group most affected by the Reagan cuts was the "working poor," a group that Reagan has consistently believed should

[7]Martin Anderson, *Welfare, The Political Economy of Welfare Reform in the United States* (Stanford, Calif.: Hoover Institution, 1978), p. 43.
[8]*Ibid.*

be weaned from the welfare system. The designation "working poor" refers to able-bodied persons of working age who have some earnings from employment and also receive federally assisted income transfers.

The working poor were affected by a number of important policy changes made in the 1981 Omnibus Budget Reconciliation Act. While the impact of these changes is hard to measure, the available evidence indicates that it is their cumulative impact that is most notable. A study of the early effects of the Reagan domestic program conducted by the Princeton Urban and Regional Research Center in fourteen states and fourteen local areas found many examples of this cumulative effect. In Cuyahoga County, Ohio, which overlies Cleveland, for example:

> About 4,000 adults in Cuyahoga County have been taken off the welfare rolls; in some cases, so have their children. Virtually no job training or placement exists to assist them in a transition to work. Their food stamp allotment will most likely be cut in coming months. Their children will have even lower chances than before of getting special attention in the Cleveland public schools; their public transportation costs have already gone up 50 percent and will rise again during 1982. Many of them may lose some medicaid benefits.[9]

THE REAGAN PROGRAM FOR FISCAL YEAR 1983

Reagan's program for fiscal year 1983 repeated the previous year's pattern by increasing the share of federal spending going to defense and cutting spending on domestic—and particularly social—programs. An analysis by the Congressional Budget Office (summarized in Table 5-3) shows defense rising from one-quarter to one-third of total federal spending over the five-year period between 1981 and 1985. Social security spending was also projected to rise in proportion to other federal outlays. Welfare payments to individuals (i.e., not counting social security as in line 4) and other nondefense spending (line 5) were predicted to fall as a share of the budget, the latter sharply.

The 1983 budget request also proposed seven new block grants for fiscal year 1983, involving the consolidation of forty-nine programs and $6.8 billion in outlays. As in the prior year, the newly proposed grant consolidations placed administrative responsibility at the state level. Yet, the 1983 budget was not entirely negative for local governments. No change in funding was proposed for two of the biggest programs providing federal aid to localities—general revenue sharing and the community development block grant program.

---

[9]Richard P. Nathan, Philip M. Dearborn, Clifford A. Goldman, and associates, "Initial Effects of the Fiscal Year 1982 Reductions in Federal Domestic Spending," in *Reductions in U.S. Domestic Spending: How They Affect State and Local Governments*, John W. Ellwood, ed. (New Brunswick, N.J.: Transaction Books, 1982), pp. 333–34.

Table 5-3 Composition of Federal Outlays, Fiscal Years 1981-1985
(percentage distribution)

	Actual	Budgeted	Administration Estimates		
	1981	1982	1983	1984	1985
National defense	24.3%	25.9%	29.2%	31.4%	33.6%
Social security	21.0	21.3	22.9	23.4	23.3
Net interest	10.5	11.4	12.7	12.2	11.6
Other payments to individuals	27.2	27.1	25.4	24.4	23.9
Other nondefense	17.1	14.2	9.8	8.6	7.6
Total	100.0%	100.0%	100.0%	100.0%	100.0%
Memorandum:					
Billions of dollars	678.2	745.0	773.3	820.2	879.4

Source: Congressional Budget Office, *An Analysis of the President's Budgetary Proposals for Fiscal Year 1983*, February 1982, table 2.6.

The administration's role in the budget process was not as dramatic and visible for 1983 as it had been for 1982. The outcome, however, was similar in many respects. About the same amount of reductions was enacted. Most of the cuts came in domestic—and particularly social—programs, and the deficit continued to soar.

REAGAN'S FEDERALISM GRAND DESIGN

Apparently not content with the devolution achieved in his first year of office, Reagan in his 1982 state of the union message proposed significant restructuring of governmental responsibilities.[10] The new plan, which was to go into effect over seven years between 1984 and 1991, proposed realignments of programs totaling $46.6 billion. The central features of the plan are what the president called *swaps* and *turnbacks*. These recommendations harked back to a proposal Reagan had made in New Hampshire in his 1976 primary campaign against Gerald Ford, calling for the elimination of $90 billion in domestic programs on the condition that state governments would be assigned the revenue sources to take over the functions involved.

The *swap* part of Reagan's 1982 plan resembled Nixon's New Federalism in that there was to be a sorting-out process, with some functions devolved and some centralized. However, important elements of the Reagan plan (particularly the way welfare was treated) were very different from what Nixon had advocated. In the Reagan plan, the federal government would assume responsibility for the medicaid program (it provides medical care for the poor) and in

[10]See Document 9.

(Bob Englehart, *Hartford Courant*. Reprinted by permission.)

exchange the states would assume the responsibility for the AFDC and food stamp programs. This proposal would be a fundamental shift for federalism, and was a major shift for Ronald Reagan. In his 1982 budget revisions, and in fact for a long time before that, Reagan had advocated that the medicaid program be devolved to the states, in essence as a block grant. Now, Reagan was proposing that medicaid be taken over by the federal government.

Reagan's plan also broke new ground for national policy in the way it proposed to treat AFDC and food stamps.[11] Since the New Deal, the federal government had taken more and more responsibility—both for policymaking and financing—for income-transfer programs. Although Nixon's family assistance plan was not enacted, Congress did enact his proposal for the supplemental security income (SSI) program. SSI gave the responsibility to the Social Security Administration for welfare programs to aid the aged, blind, and disabled, which had previously been administered by the states and by local governments. Also, in the Nixon years, the food stamp program was greatly expanded and became a uniform national program financed entirely by the federal government.

[11]See Document 7.

Reagan's proposal to devolve the food stamp program to the states was the most radical shift for federalism advanced in the 1982 state of the union message. The food stamp program, from its inception, has been predominantly a national program, whereas the AFDC program has always involved divided responsibilities. The food stamp proposal was short-lived, however. In April 1982, three months after it had been put forward, Reagan abandoned the idea in response to strong opposition that emerged during negotiations with state and local officials.

In contrast, state and local officials approved of Reagan's proposal to centralize responsibility for the medicaid program. As one of Lyndon Johnson's Great Society programs, medicaid grew from $3.2 billion in 1970 to $12.5 billion in 1980. Spending under medicaid is difficult to control, because anyone in several categories—including AFDC recipients—is eligible to have medicaid costs paid under the program. Because states pay about half the program's cost, the growth in expenditures has put many states in a financial bind. While the news that the federal government would take over this responsibility was welcome, state officials and health experts generally expressed concern about the administration's failure to specify what medical services the federal government would provide, who would be aided, and on what basis.

The swap was only part of Reagan's 1982 grand design for reforming American federalism. The plan also called for establishing a trust fund to finance so-called *turnback* programs, which would be devolved to the states. The forty-four programs originally listed in the 1983 budget as "illustrative" of those to be turned back to the states included 125 separate grants-in-aid. Besides the revenue sharing program, which was on the "turnback list," the major functional areas affected were education, employment and training, social services, public health, transportation (though not interstate highways), and community development.

Finally, the federal government was to relinquish certain taxes to the states to help them pay for the programs "turned back" to them. The federal taxes to be relinquished included alcohol, tobacco, and telephone excise taxes; two cents per gallon of the gasoline tax; and a portion of the windfall profits tax on energy resources. These federal taxes are eventually scheduled to be terminated. In the meantime, however, the money was to be distributed to the states. The basic idea underlying these proposals was that no state would win or lose from the swap and turnback initiatives taken as a whole.

The reactions to Reagan's 1982 reform plan, although they varied from state to state, were generally cool. Despite intensive efforts to negotiate a version of the Reagan plan that would be acceptable to state and local government officials, agreement was slow in coming. The necessary enabling legislation was not transmitted to the Congress in time for consideration in the 97th Congress.

Debate within the Reagan administration on this plan became heated, and—rare for this administration—even public.[12] The result was a victory for conservatives within the administration. The negotiations were directed by Richard A. Williamson, assistant to the president for intergovernmental relations, who at times seemed on the verge of working out a plan with state and local officials (primarily state officials) that could pass muster within the administration. However, the failure of the governors to sign up, and the covert and overt internal opposition to the Williamson plan by White House aide Robert Carleson, OMB Director Stockman, and others led the administration to abandon its hopes of having a legislative package to submit in 1982.

THE LEGISLATIVE PROGRAM

Although much less successful in the second year than in the first, the Reagan administration was able to achieve a bold legislative program, mainly through the congressional budget process. Three explanations for this success appear to be important at this juncture. The most important change in procedural terms was the use of the reconciliation process to revise the federal budget. In this way the administration was able to win in a single vote what amounted to omnibus domestic legislation. A second explanation is the change in national mood on domestic issues. Retrenchment was gaining ground steadily in the 1970s beginning at the local level. A third explanation has to do with the administration's "supply-side" economic policy. The $737 billion five-year tax cut enacted in 1981 put pressure on the federal budget and made it easier to win support for domestic policy changes implemented through the budget process.

[12]See David S. Broder, "Reagan's Bold Stroke Went Wild," *Trenton Times*, August 11, 1982, p. A-9.

CHAPTER 6

Administrative Tactics Under Reagan

The Reagan administration's efforts to change the operations of the federal bureaucracy have been just as noteworthy as the legislative and budgetary changes discussed in the last chapter.

The key ingredient has been the appointment of loyal and committed policy officials. But this is only one dimension. The internal organization and operation of the White House staff is another. Loyal "Reaganites" have been placed in key White House policymaking positions, with experienced Washington hands assigned to parallel posts to promote the administration's policies in the legislative process and in the media. Tensions between the White House staff and cabinet officers have been minimized through the use of cabinet councils in which cabinet members have an important policymaking role. Appointed policy officials in agency posts have penetrated administrative operations by grabbing hold of spending, regulatory, and personnel decisions. From the beginning, these and other administrative tactics have been used aggressively by the Reagan administration.

The information contained in this chapter is based on interviews, library research, and a working knowledge of a number of domestic agencies. However, I was not an on-the-scene observer as I was during the Nixon first term. Research from a distance is not the same thing as being there. Besides, it is early in the story—two years into the Reagan presidency—to make final judgments on the success or failure of the administrative tactics of the Reagan administration.

INTERNAL ORGANIZATION

The internal organization of the executive office is crucial to the workings of any administration. The Nixon administration, as earlier chapters pointed out, was haunted by organizational weaknesses. Development of the counter-bureaucracy is only one example of decision-making apparatus gone awry. Other presidents have also been plagued by an ineffective organization. In a recent book, two top aides in the Carter administration warn:

> The EOP [Executive Office of the President] has suffered for a decade from serious weaknesses. It has become too big, containing too many staffs and advisors peripheral to its central functions. It has always been structured in a confusing manner, inviting internal conflicts over decision-making, advice-giving and coordinating authority. Its operating procedures have been haphazard, unfair and easily "gamed." Its inability to make decisions short of the President has led to delay, uncertainty and presidential overload. And it has lacked a strategic center able to marshal the forces of executive government so that the President can get done what he wants done.[1]

Learning from the experience of its predecessors, the Reagan administration has effectively organized the functions of the executive office and the relationships between the executive office staff and cabinet and subcabinet officials. Cabinet officers, through their work in the cabinet councils, have a visible policymaking role, but the major staff responsibility for these councils lies within the White House. Another important feature of the Reagan approach is the appointment of subcabinet officials who are more doctrinaire and at the same time much less visible than their cabinet superiors. The result has been that many of the strongest administrative actions, as discussed later in this chapter, have not received controversial front-page national publicity.

The internal workings of the Reagan White House staff in the first two years centered on the triumvirate of Edwin Meese III, James Baker III, and Michael Deaver. At least in the early part of the administration this group has been distinguished by the unusually close working relationships among its members. Counselor to the President Edwin Meese has had the lead role on substance, having served Reagan the longest, and as a result was most closely attuned to his ideas and attitudes on policy matters. As chief of staff, Baker has been responsible for management. Deaver has been responsible for scheduling for the president and is the lead advisor on political matters involving long-time presidential associates. But the lines are not rigid. The strength of

[1]Heineman and Hessler, *op. cit.*, pp. 11–12. For a discussion of the Executive Office of the President, see also Walter Williams, "Strangers and Brothers: The Dilemma of Organizing and Staffing the American Presidency," Discussion Paper 5 (Seattle: Institute for Public Policy and Management, University of Washington, April 1981).

the Reagan troika system is the understanding among four people—Reagan, Meese, Baker, and Deaver.

The smooth functioning to date of the White House policy apparatus on the domestic side is also attributable to an important though not overly rigid delineation between policymaking and policy implementation. The organizational structure of the White House has preserved the Reagan philosophy by placing the policymaking apparatus—the Office of Policy Development—under the control of Meese, a Reagan aide of long standing whose point of view is closely in line with Reagan's. (This Office of Policy Development has responsibilities similar to the Domestic Council under Nixon.)

At the same time, the Reagan White House has been able to avoid the "outsider" image that plagued the Carter administration by bringing people with Washington experience into the White House to handle implementation tasks, which come under the general aegis of James Baker. An insider's knowledge is particularly valuable in such tasks as congressional relations. An experienced staff consisting of a number of Capitol Hill veterans has been assembled by the Reagan administration. One long-time Republican described the Reagan congressional relations team as "the best we've seen in recent years, since LBJ's guys operated up here."[2]

The troika of Reagan aides is backed up by an information system run by Richard Darman, who reports formally to Baker and is responsible for managing the White House staff, and Craig Fuller, who reports to Meese and is responsible for White House-cabinet relations. They work very closely together in administering a computerized information system for White House decision making. The system is said to have logged 11,000 memoranda and comments in the first year of the Reagan presidency.

Reagan's normal schedule is to be in the Oval Office from 9:00 to 5:30 four days a week, from 9:00 until 1:00 on a fifth day, and rarely on weekends. He does paper work (reviewing decision and briefing memos and speech drafts) for an average of about two hours each evening in the residence.

Much more so than its predecessors, the Reagan system for dealing with domestic affairs has for the most part been a harmonious one.[3] Part of the reason is no doubt that the administration is ideologically based. It has a clear direction. There are, according to one aide, "few pragmatists floating around."

Another reason for this cohesion has to do with the budget. Budget exi-

[2]See Dick Kirschten, "The Pennsylvania Ave. Connection—Making Peace on Capitol Hill," *National Journal*, March 7, 1981, p. 384.

[3]During the Reagan administration's second year, some observers detected signs of serious emerging tensions among the members of the troika and their respective staffs, especially between Meese and Baker. See Jack Nelson, "Infighting Racks Reagan Advisers," *Los Angeles Times*, August 15, 1982, p. 1. See also William Greider, "Reagan's Twilight Zone," *Rolling Stone*, September 16, 1982, p. 11.

gencies (some self-inflicted as a consequence of the 1981 tax cut) have resulted in a high premium on budget cutting, especially for domestic programs. The skillful leadership of David Stockman, director of the Office of Management and Budget, has contributed to what appears to be a partial eclipse of the domestic policy apparatus in the White House under Reagan.[4] Budget decisions have been the drive wheel of policy, with domestic issues often subordinated to the budget process.

CABINET COUNCILS

Unlike Nixon, Reagan came to office with experience as an executive of a large organization (the state of California), and, unlike Carter (who was also a governor), he had clear ideas regarding the role of the cabinet and had a reputation as a skillful delegator.

The evidence suggests that he had decided to put his management philosophy into effect at the very start of his administration. Speaking to the International Business Council in Chicago in September 1980, Reagan said, "Crucial to my strategy of spending control will be the appointment to top government positions of men and women who share my economic philosophy. We will have an administration in which the word from the top isn't lost or hidden in the bureaucracy. That voice will be heard because it is the voice of the people."[5] On the night before the election, Reagan is quoted as saying it was his intention to bring about "a new structuring of the presidential cabinet that will make cabinet officers the managers of the national administration—not captives of the bureaucracy or special interests they are supposed to direct."[6]

Admittedly, such statements do nothing more than suggest presidential intent. But it is clear that President Reagan envisioned a role for his cabinet much different from that envisioned by President Nixon in his first term. A *National Journal* analysis in February 1981 stated, "The role of Cabinet officers and senior appointed officials is to function as loyal lieutenants dedicated to the pursuit of presidential objectives."[7]

In one important respect, Reagan's organizational arrangement for domestic affairs resembles Nixon's approach, namely, the use of cabinet councils

---

[4]Martin Anderson, Reagan's first director of the White House domestic policy staff, left in the spring of 1982. He had a long association with Reagan and was instrumental in developing the policies of the early period of Reagan's presidency. His role after the early rounds of policy decisions, however, was less successful. He was succeeded by Edwin Harper, a former White House official for domestic policy in the Nixon administration and deputy director of the Office of Management and Budget immediately prior to his move into the Nixon White House.

[5]Transcript reprinted in *New York Times*, September 19, 1980.

[6]*New York Times*, March 8, 1981.

[7]Dick Kirschten: "Reagan: No More Business as Usual," *National Journal*, February 21, 1981, p. 300.

for major functional areas of domestic policy. Although these councils meet frequently, they have not caused the kind of friction that arose under Nixon at meetings of the Urban Affairs Council staffed by Daniel Patrick Moynihan.

Reagan named five cabinet councils in addition to the National Security Council, which is required by law. They are on economic affairs, commerce and trade, human resources, natural resources and environment, and food and agriculture. According to media accounts and based on interviews, the cabinet councils' work is conducted in three phases. Issues begin at the lowest level. The staff secretariat, made up of representatives of each of the council members and chaired by staff from the Office of Policy Development, writes policy papers. Next, cabinet-level working sessions, chaired by the designated secretary, refine the issues. Finally, policy decisions are made in sessions often chaired by the president.[8]

The councils met about 150 times in the first year, with the president attending about a third of the meetings. The most active group was the council on economic affairs, chaired by Treasury Secretary Donald T. Regan. The Darman-Fuller information system is closely tied to the work of the councils. Meese and Baker attend council meetings when the president does, and occasionally at other times. The Office of Management and Budget is represented on all the councils.

There is some controversy as to whether the councils are paper organizations and ratifiers or whether they are genuinely involved in decision making.[9] On the whole, it seems that the councils are active and do make many decisions. The reason that they operate more effectively than past decision processes in the White House traces to the appointments process and the fact that the officials in the Reagan administration have such a strong set of shared ideological positions.

Scientist Niels Bohr is reported to have said, "Prediction is very difficult, especially about the future." If one were to try to predict what might happen to the Reagan policymaking apparatus, its vulnerability may be the tendency, discernible in interviews and newspaper reports, for participants to regard the cabinet-council system as so effective that it can handle any issue. There appears to be a lack of appreciation of the danger, as indicated in Chapter 3, in what Robert Wood calls the "curious inversion," whereby the more the White House tries to do, the less it can do. Success—that is, the success of the cabinet-council system—could end up, if carried too far, in undermining the Reagan system.

[8]Dick Kirschten, "Circles Within Circles," *National Journal*, March 7, 1981, p. 399.

[9]Writing in *The Washington Post*, Lou Cannon and David Hoffman downplay the role of the cabinet councils. They note that dominance by the White House is "accepted—even applauded—by members of the Reagan cabinet noted more for its fealty than its independence." See Lou Cannon and David Hoffman, "The Inner Circle Decides and the Outer Circle Ratifies," *The Washington Post*, July 18, 1982, p. 1.

THE APPOINTMENTS PROCESS

The essence of the Reagan approach to management is the appointment of loyal and determined policy officials. This, of course, is not a new idea; the difference is that the Reagan administration has in substantial measure carried it out.

Six months before the 1980 presidential campaign got under way, steps were taken to plan a system for appointing persons to cabinet and major subcabinet posts. The selection process for presidential appointments was designed by Edwin Meese and E. Pendleton James, a White House personnel aide under Nixon who became director of personnel in the Reagan White House. Although under steady fire from the Republican right wing, James served through July 1982, during which period he had an office in the White House, held a Level II appointment (cabinet officers are Level I), and had regular access to the president. According to G. Calvin MacKenzie, of the Department of Government at Colby College, James "provided an unprecedented thread of consistency throughout the entire staffing of the Reagan administration" as "the most stalwart protector . . . of a policy of centralized control of presidential appointments."[10]

James and his principal aide and successor, Helene Von Damm, and a staff of about ten professionals were responsible for selecting the 430 men and women who received presidential appointments in the Reagan administration as cabinet and subcabinet officials. They met at least once a week with the Meese-Baker-Deaver troika in the early days, more often if necessary. Cabinet members were consulted on all subcabinet appointments. The president was personally involved in discussions of appointments to all cabinet posts and in cases where the White House group and the cabinet secretary differed on a particular subcabinet appointment. The aim was to find persons who would "rock the boat"—who would not be unduly tied to the status quo. Three to four names were sought as finalists for each post. Interviews with eight to ten people who knew each candidate were instrumental in the decision process. Each new appointee was carefully briefed by White House officials in preparation for confirmation hearings in the Senate.

Compared with his recent predecessors, the Reagan administration took a long time to fill cabinet and subcabinet positions. The delays were a function both of new procedural steps growing out of the new conflict-of-interest law, which requires additional steps in the clearance process, and the care taken to find committed Reaganites who would accept federal salaries, which by 1981 had been seriously eroded by inflation. Nevertheless, by mid-1981, Howell

[10]G. Calvin MacKenzie, "The Reaganites Come To Town: Personnel Selection for a Conservative Administration," paper presented at the 1981 Convention of the American Political Science Association, processed, p. 5.

Raines was able to write in the *New York Times* about "a revolution of attitudes involving the appointment of officials who in previous administrations might have been ruled out by concern over possible lack of qualifications or conflict of interest, or open hostility to the mission of the agencies they now lead."[11] Raines cited the following examples:

- In appointments, regulatory jobs important to business were filled months ago, while key positions in agencies aimed at guaranteeing the rights of minorities, consumers, workers, and union members have been filled only in the last few weeks or remain vacant.
- In regulatory agencies, most appointees are former employees or financial beneficiaries of the concerns whose activities they are supposed to police. But appointees to agencies that guard individual rights often have records of little or no experience, philosophical neutrality, or proven opposition to the missions of the agencies they direct.
- Stewardship of natural resources on Federal lands has been turned over to former employees of mining, timber, and oil companies, while environmental quality jobs have gone to advocates of increased use of coal and nuclear power and of lower water and air quality standards for industry.[12]

Not only are Reagan's cabinet and subcabinet officials ideologically in tune with their chief, many of them in the domestic agencies have managerial experience and a willingness, if not a desire, to apply this experience in government.

To assure and maintain the ideological purity of the cabinet and subcabinet, the Reagan White House has relied on training or indoctrination activities to an unusually high degree. During the transition, cabinet members learned about their departments from conservative task forces rather than from personnel within their agencies. Cabinet appointees also met frequently with Reagan in this early period so that they would get "used to working with him" before developing close ties with their department staff.[13] Cabinet meetings, especially in the early days, were used more for indoctrination than to discuss policy issues or decide policy options. (The cabinet councils fill this policy-making function.) Three to four breakfast meetings have been held for large groups of subcabinet appointees each year. Reagan, Vice-President Bush, Treasury Secretary Regan, OMB Director Stockman, and senior White House officials have been the main speakers at these breakfasts.

[11] Howell Raines, "Reagan Reversing Many U.S. Policies," *New York Times*, July 3, 1981.
[12] *Ibid.*
[13] As quoted in Kirschten, "Reagan: No More Business as Usual," p. 302.

The Reagan administration also took an unprecedented interest in the lower-level political positions within the executive branch. In addition to cabinet and subcabinet appointees, there are two personnel categories that can be controlled by an administration. One is Schedule C or exempt positions, which generally provide administrative and staff support for higher-level political appointees. There are approximately 1,300 such positions. The second category includes approximately 700 persons in the senior civil service who have noncareer status. Since the enactment of the 1978 Civil Service Act, these positions have been explicitly controllable by an administration through demotion, transfer, or removal.

Prior administrations have taken little if any interest in middle- and lower-level positions. In at least one period during their administration, both Presidents Nixon and Carter explicitly turned the selection of subcabinet positions over to their cabinets. This has not been true of the Reagan administration. From the beginning it was clear that subcabinet positions, in particular, would be controlled by the White House. Members of the cabinet were, however, consulted and involved in subcabinet appointments. In exchange, the White House asked to be consulted in the same way by cabinet members on all Schedule C and senior civil service appointments.

OTHER ADMINISTRATIVE TACTICS

Reagan's appointees have been involved in administrative processes in other ways besides personnel selection and indoctrination. The most important involves the review—and approval or disapproval—of spending decisions. At the outset of the administration, the administration's appointees in many domestic agencies put all spending projects in the pipeline on ''hold.'' Review processes were launched that resulted in shifting contracts and grants to recipients felt to be in agreement with Reagan's conservative policies. Major projects that had been developed under Carter and had a liberal cast were disapproved. The funds recouped were used in other ways or simply allowed to lapse. (In the latter case, the law requires that a rescission action be approved by Congress; some reprogramming decisions also require congressional approval.) Tactics of this kind have been used consistently and effectively by the Reagan administration in ways that had appreciable impact and are unusual for Washington.

Regulatory action is another area where Reagan's cabinet and subcabinet officials exerted major influence in administrative processes. Deregulation was a major announced aim of the Reagan administration, as it had been under Carter. The difference was that, while Carter achieved some notable legislative successes in this area, his appointees did not pursue deregulation through administrative action.

Under Reagan, federal regulatory changes—particularly the removal of existing regulations and the relaxation of their enforcement—have been used as an important instrument of policy redirection. The main arena of regulatory change, however, was the private rather than the public sector. The Reagan administration has used deregulation primarily to remove barriers and red tape that it felt restricted business activities. To a more limited extent, deregulation also has been used as an instrument for devolution in the field of domestic policy, especially to remove "strings" on state and local governments under federal grants-in-aid. In this area, however, the creation of block grants through legislative action has been the more prominent approach. In fact, there have been important cases in the welfare and environmental areas where the Reagan administration has increased the regulations on states and localities as a means of putting other domestic policies into effect.[14]

A third type of administrative tactic used skillfully by Reagan cabinet and subcabinet appointees involves personnel management. Reagan appointees have been adept in taking advantage of opportunities to transfer and remove career officials in domestic agencies felt to be unsympathetic to the administration's objectives. "Reductions in force" (RIFs) were carried out in many agencies. In the Labor Department, for example, a RIF notice was sent to the entire management staff of the Employment and Training Administration. After the required notice period had elapsed, large numbers of persons were terminated. The dividing line in seniority for these layoffs was fifteen years of service in some units. Persons with less service were laid off. Many who stayed on were reduced in grade, with the result that some very senior civil servants were assigned to routine tasks with no substantive content.

In the case of the Commerce Department's Economic Development Administration, where the authorizing law had expired and the Reagan budget proposed abolishing the agency, the administration sought to eliminate the agency's entire staff. The result was that when Congress appropriated a limited amount of money for the Economic Development Administration in fiscal year 1982, keeping it barely alive, its staff was dispersed and discouraged and the program languished as a result.

The 1978 Civil Service Reform Act passed under Carter and hailed by him as a management advance, as already indicated, turned out to be an effective instrument under Reagan. Officials in the new senior civil service who have noncareer status can be replaced by an incoming administration or cabinet sec-

---

[14]For further discussion of this subject, see Catherine Lovell, "Federal Deregulation and State and Local Governments," in John W. Ellwood, ed., *Reductions in U.S. Domestic Spending: How They Affect State and Local Governments* (New Brunswick, N.J.: Transaction Books, 1982).

DOONESBURY   **by Garry Trudeau**

retary. Few who were in this status were kept on under Reagan. In retrospect, White House officials indicated that in their view the best and clearest approach is to remove and replace all such persons as a matter of course and without exception. While some proponents of civil service reform saw these types of changes as a perversion of the system, it can be argued that the new law is working exactly the way it should, despite the pain involved for persons removed from office.

On a more general basis, the Reagan administration has taken steps to slow down the growth of the bureaucracy. The president promised in his inaugural address to "curb the size and influence of the Federal establishment."[15] On taking office, he ordered a freeze on federal hiring. Exceptions have been made sparingly since the freeze was lifted in mid-1981.

AGENCY EXAMPLES

Increasingly, media and public comment has focused on the administrative system of the Reagan administration and its relations with the bureaucracy. Many examples can be found where Reagan appointees successfully took on the bureaucracy to pursue the administration's policy goals. An almost competitive relationship existed in these terms between Interior Secretary James Watt and Anne Gorsuch, administrator of the Environmental Protection Agency. The end result was that the environmental policies of the prior fifteen years were substantially diluted. Watt opened up federal lands to coal and timber exploration and recreational uses, and sharply increased contracting for offshore oil drilling. Gorsuch cut the budget and staff of her agency and relaxed the enforcement of federal regulations to prevent and reduce air and water pollution; she also changed some of the regulations themselves.

[15]See Document 8.

Early in the administration Watt came across as especially heavy-handed. When he characterized Washington as divided between "liberals and Americans," a corporate lobbyist active in Democratic politics criticized the secretary for this remark; the lobbyist was removed from his position, reportedly as a result of Watt's intervention.[16] Gorsuch at EPA was less public at the outset but got headlines for proposing drastic budget cuts for her agency and producing what critics termed a "talent hemorrhage." The *National Journal* reported that about 2,500 full-time employees were expected to depart voluntarily from the EPA during the first two years of the Reagan administration.[17]

Other Reagan appointees have behaved the same way, but with less fanfare. In the Labor Department, Assistant Secretary Albert Angrisani, who has kept out of the limelight, took control of the department's employment and training programs in an unprecedented way. On taking office, Angrisani suspended all grants and contracts that were in the pipeline and allowed none of them to go into effect without his personal approval. He drastically cut the personnel level of the Employment and Training Administration, the largest operating unit in the Labor Department, and one that in the past had a high level of funding and was assigned major social-policy objectives. Angrisani transferred and downgraded veteran staffers of the Employment and Training Administration, and in countless strong actions asserted his ideas throughout the agency. A former banker, he complained about the past record of employment and training programs as "seven years of mismanagement practices." He sought to make manpower training programs, in his words, "lean and mean."[18]

Angrisani's actions are typical of the steps taken by Reagan subcabinet appointees. These officials have tended to be more doctrinaire Reaganites than their cabinet superiors. Cabinet secretaries, on the other hand, have tended to be more conciliatory. Hence, media attention on encounters between Reagan appointees and the bureaucracy is more subdued than would be the case if the more visible cabinet members—Watt is a notable exception—were involved in agency infighting.

In the welfare field, for example, a triumvirate of former California Reagan aides appointed to key posts below the cabinet level came to play a dominant role both in policy and administration. While Secretary Schweiker

[16]Phil Gailey, "Democratic Lawyers Finding Interior Cold," *New York Times*, February 2, 1982. Watt's tactics are seen by some observers as having backfired because they caused so much new interest in and support for the work of environmental activists and organizations. This is also true, but less so, of Anne Gorsuch.

[17]Lawrence Mosher, "Move Over, Jim Watt, Anne Gorsuch Is the Latest Target of Environmentalists," *National Journal*, October 24, 1981, p. 1900.

[18]William J. Lanouette, "Life After Death—CETA's Demise Won't Mean the End of Manpower Training," *National Journal*, February 6, 1982, p. 241.

appears to be generally supportive of their activities, he also tends to act, and to be portrayed in the press, as more moderate.

The welfare-policy triumvirate all have strong Reagan credentials. Robert Carleson, a White House aide, is the intellectual leader of the group. The two other members are David B. Swoap, undersecretary of the Department of Health and Human Services, and John A. Svahn, commissioner of the large and powerful Social Security Administration. Each of the three served at one time as welfare director in California under Reagan. A newspaper article on the influence of this trio stated, "Not only do they have a long and close working association with Mr. Reagan and one another but also, by virtue of their work in California and later with Federal welfare agencies and welfare committees on Capitol Hill, they tend to have a more detailed bureaucratic knowledge about social programs than does Mr. Schweiker, a former Senator from Pennsylvania."[19]

Carleson, Svahn, and Swoap get major credit for the dramatic changes in welfare policies contained in the 1981 budget reconciliation act, especially the systematic and successful effort described in Chapter 5 to remove the working poor from the welfare rolls. They have also been successful in influencing administrative decision making and procedures and personnel assignments in the welfare area.

Similar, though less aggressive, efforts were made to assert control over the housing and community development programs of the Department of Housing and Urban Development. Regulations for the agency's large and important block grant program for community development (over $3 billion per year) had been tightened by President Carter in order to target these funds on distressed neighborhoods and the poor. Under Reagan, changes were made in the law in 1981 to loosen the targeting requirements. But more important than these legal changes, HUD Secretary Samuel Pierce reduced the department's oversight activities and staff. The administrative actions turned HUD back to the "hands off" policy that had prevailed when the program was first enacted under Gerald Ford.

IMPACT ON OFFICIAL WASHINGTON

The net effect of controlling the bureaucracy through administrative actions has been a decided change in tone in official Washington. Agency morale has plummeted as jobs have been cut out and changed. The threat of being laid off or downgraded has had a pervasive effect among federal employees. Career officers have been required to clear all decisions with their appointed superiors.

[19]Robert Pear, "Three Key Aides Reshape Welfare Policy," *The New York Times*, April 26, 1982, p. B-8.

They have been prohibited from discussing policy matters with outside groups. The most decided change in tone and mood, as one would expect, has been in the domestic agencies.

As is often the case, an anecdote helps to make this point about the change in official Washington. In mid-1982, the *New York Times* reported that staff of the Department of Energy tried to recruit employees to attend a White House-sponsored rally in support of the balanced budget amendment to the Constitution at which the president was to speak. They were singularly unsuccessful. Citing the possibility of reductions in force and the president's plan to abolish the Energy Department, the *Times* account reported that "workers in some offices hooted and jeered the recruiters."[20]

This incident highlights a potential Achilles' heel of the Reagan administration. As Hugh Heclo reminds us, there is a delicate balance between controlling and managing the bureaucracy:

> Political figures who hope to lead Washington's bureaucracies face the fundamental problem of trying to generate the changes they want without losing the bureaucratic services they need. They have to learn not only how to help themselves but also how to acquire help from the powerful and valuable subordinates in their own organizations. Mere control of personnel—having my guy on the job—will not necessarily produce control of programs or improve government performance. One reason is that an appointed political loyalist may not know what to do, or how to do it, or when to stop doing it and check back for new guidance. A second and even more important reason is that real political control (rather than just the temporary appearance of it) depends on access to continuous capabilities in government—civil "services" that are provided not so much out of personal loyalty as out of institutionalized responsiveness.[21]

All things considered, the Reagan administration has been successful in advancing its domestic policy goals during its first two years of office. It is especially noteworthy that its policy goals were advanced through a *dual approach* that includes both legislative and administrative tactics. Regardless of what the Reagan administration will face in the future, it has already left a distinct imprint on the federal establishment.

---

[20]"Briefing," *New York Times*, July 22, 1982, p. B-6

[21]Hugh Heclo, *A Government of Strangers: Executive Politics in Washington* (Washington, D.C.: The Brookings Institution, 1977), p. 235.

CHAPTER 7

Lessons and Prospects

This final chapter draws on the experience of Nixon and Reagan and other recent presidents to consider the future role of political officials in managing the federal government. It concentrates, as does the book as a whole, on the role of the elected chief executive.

An elected chief executive has several roles. The president, a governor, or a mayor of a large city is many things—politician, strategist, spokesperson, ceremonial head of government, and publicist all rolled into one. The point of this book is not that elected chief executives should be managers in the sense of running the day-to-day affairs of government. Rather, it is that such officials should organize their office—appoint, assign, and motivate their principal appointees—in a way that *penetrates* the administrative process. The reason is that in a complex, technologically advanced society in which the role of government is pervasive, much of what we would define as policymaking is done through the execution of laws in the management process.

THE MANAGEMENT PROCESS

When politicians talk about improving management in government, they often appear to believe, rather naively, that business executives should be put in charge of major agencies. They believe that, through the implementation of business techniques, these executives will efficiently perform such managerial tasks as getting the mail delivered on time, having the trains run on schedule, cleaning up the subways, developing new sources of energy, and getting chiselers off welfare. The problem with this approach is that there are fundamental differences between the public and private sectors. These differences must be taken into account when implementing an administrative strategy.

Professor Robert Anthony of the Harvard Business School distinguishes between two kinds of control processes in business.[1] One is *"strategic planning,"* which according to Anthony is creative and episodic. In strategic planning, top managers decide what the firm's objectives should be and what resources it should use to attain those objectives. Should the firm introduce a new product, buy a new plant, declare a dividend? Such decisions, according to Anthony, are made by a small group of the highest officials.

The second major type of business-control process for Anthony is *"management control,"* which is carried out on a narrower basis in what are called "responsibility centers." Within responsibility centers in a particular firm, line managers mobilize people and resources to carry out the objectives set by the top executives.

Anthony's concept of strategic planning carried out at the highest level of an organization by a small group of senior officials does not transfer readily to the public sector. Government is much less hierarchical and much more pluralistic than business. The line between strategic planning and management control in government cannot be drawn so easily. Sometimes it cannot be drawn at all. The reason for this is simple: *Strategy or policy (as it is often called, in the public sector) consists of those decisions that people consider important because they affect values that are basic and controversial.*

Strategic decisions in government cannot be distinguished from management decisions on the basis of their generality. Examples help to make this point. Quite detailed decisions—such as those on the books used for sex education in the high schools, on the types of jobs welfare recipients should be required to accept, on the location of highways, or on the deployment of police officers in a large city—frequently involve many participants in a highly competitive setting. Often, if they become sufficiently controversial, decisions of this character can involve the highest-ranking political officials, including the elected chief executive.

To summarize, administrative processes in the public and private sectors are organized and conducted differently because of three factors: (1) the unclear and often inchoate nature of the values at stake in government, (2) the frequent lack of numerical benchmarks (such as profits and losses) against which to measure performance, and (3) the essential purpose of a democratic

---

[1] Robert N. Anthony, *Planning and Control Systems, A Framework for Analysis* (Cambridge: Harvard University Press, 1965), Chapter 1.

political system, which is to provide mechanisms for constantly adjusting governmental policies to the beliefs and preferences of the citizenry.

Because of the nature of government, there are no easy formulas for a professional manager in government. Above all, these career managers need a sophisticated understanding of how our highly pluralistic democratic system works. We require managers who operate what Anthony calls responsibility centers even though the issues involved cannot be neatly divided between "policy" and "management." Successful managers in the public sector must understand the competitive nature of the U.S. political system with all of its complexities and subtleties. They must be able to operate cheek to jowl with politicians of the highest rank. They must be able in their day-to-day activities to sort out those cases and situations that involve policy and politics and those that do not.

On the other side of the coin, appointed policy officials must become involved with the bureaucracy in administrative processes. Appointed officials in the U.S. executive branch often fail to appreciate this point. They have tended to concentrate on the strategic or policy level and avoid getting involved in messy operational matters. It is in these terms that change is most needed; political officials must seek ways to push policy (the ideas they were elected or selected to advance) into administrative processes. This is the essence of the administrative presidency strategy.

Wallace S. Sayre, professor of public administration at Columbia University, had a favorite device for describing policymaking in government. He described government as a wheel with many spokes. The "hub" in his model was the career bureau chief. The bureau chief receives policy signals from many sources, which are the "spokes" of Sayre's wheel of government. Among these sources are the president, his cabinet, the courts, the career staff of the chief's own bureau, the Congress and its committees and staff, interest groups, political parties, other bureaus, and the media.[2] Each of these actors in the political process may interact with the bureau chief at any given time and influence his or her behavior. Under certain conditions, the wishes of a particular actor or set of actors will have greater immediate or long-range importance to the bureau chief than those of the president or a member of his cabinet.

The point of Sayre's model is that participants in a governmental decision process (including presidents) need to view their role as only one of many actors endeavoring to influence governmental decision making. This is not a new point. It is most often associated with the writing of Richard Neustadt. Neustadt portrays the president as one of many actors attempting to influence

[2]Walter G. Held, *Decisionmaking in the Federal Government: The Wallace S. Sayre Model* (Washington, D.C.: The Brookings Institution, 1979).

other actors in the political process.[3] While the president has an especially strong claim as the highest elected official of the executive branch, he cannot call all of the shots. He is not the president of General Motors. Members of Congress, the courts, and many other actors in the system of American government influence administrative processes. I do not make this point to lament the fact that the president cannot exercise full control over the bureaucracy, but rather to demonstrate that explicit effort is required if the president is to exert *greater* influence over the bureaucracy on administrative matters. The key to doing this is the role of his principal appointees in major agencies of the executive branch.

THE ROLE OF CABINET AND SUBCABINET OFFICIALS

There are, as we have seen, two main groups of presidential officials—cabinet secretaries and subcabinet officials. The first group is relatively easy to define. The second is more amorphous. It includes appointees at several levels; some have statutory posts and are confirmed by the Senate, while others are in lower posts. The subcabinet has been variously counted. The essential character of all of these political positions is that they are temporary and are tied to the fortunes of a particular administration or official.

The role of a subcabinet official in management is necessarily different from that of the secretary. *It is less general and more operational.* Management, in short, means different things to different types of executive branch officials. As one moves down the organizational ladder, political officials become more involved in administrative processes. A skillful cabinet secretary gives signals on matters involving agency operation in a very general way. This can be done in the budget process, in reviewing regulatory issuances, and in speeches or other statements. The administrative strategy of a cabinet secretary typically involves not so much being a manager as *being involved in management.*

The point is that one can view management for political officials as a progression in which each lower level of political officials needs to be closer to, and more involved in, administrative processes. All political officials, however, must be *selective.* Even lower-level appointed officials (senior civil service and Schedule C) cannot view themselves as responsible for every managerial operation of the programs and activities under their purview, for every sparrow that falls, every application or administrative ruling that goes astray. Political officials must define their roles in a way that allows them to intervene selectively in

[3]Richard E. Neustadt, *Presidential Power, The Politics of Leadership from FDR to Carter* (New York: John Wiley & Sons, Inc., 1980).

the operations of the bureaucracy on a basis that involves a workable set of continuing relationships between political and career officials. We need to look again at the role of the bureaucracy in this context.

THE ROLE OF THE BUREAUCRACY RECONSIDERED

In recent decades, much of our thinking about the role of the federal bureaucracy has been influenced by a generation of career officials who entered the government during the Great Depression. Members of this entering class of the best and brightest are now leaving the federal service, or have already left. Their service encompassed a long period of growth and activism on the part of the U.S. national government in the field of domestic affairs. The viewpoint of these federal officials tended to emphasize the planner's perspective, the systematic identification and solution of problems. This approach has its advantages in clarity and directness, but it can under some circumstances reflect a liberal bias that problems, once discovered, should be solved by government.

The tensions between appointed political officials and the bureaucracy in the Reagan and Nixon periods come down to a basic question involving the role of politicians in defining the scope and tasks of government versus the application of more academic analytical techniques of problem identification and problem solving on the part of professionals. No conclusive answer can ever be given as to which group should dominate, nor is it possible to provide a specific delineation of the proper roles of politicians and bureaucrats.

Under Reagan, this issue has come to the fore in many subtle ways. Critics of the administration claim that its approach is demoralizing for the bureaucracy because of its confrontational tactics and that this undermines the capacity of government to operate efficiently. My own view is that there is a need to strike a new balance between planning and management in the government service. In essence, this means going back toward the original meaning of the idea of "neutral competence" discussed in the first chapter.

There is an irony in this state of affairs. The tendency for planning values—problem identification and problem solving based heavily on analytical techniques—to predominate in the public service has caused mistrust of the bureaucracy on the part of conservatives and often the public generally. Efforts by professionals in government service to place more stress on management and managerial skills and the original meaning of the concept of neutral competence are likely to end up increasing public confidence in government. In the long run, such efforts are in the interests of both liberals and conservatives on domestic and social issues.

When the pendulum swings again in the 1990s—or whenever—and a new activism or liberal mood is asserted for government, it will have to be grounded in confidence in government. Building such confidence is hard work and not very dramatic, but it is essential and critical. This work must be done by those who believe that government can be a positive, constructive force in the society, worthy of being assigned new responsibilities and tasks.

THE ROLE OF THE PRESIDENT AS A MANAGER

The focus of this book is on the managerial role of the president. Among recent presidents, there have been notable failures because of two misconceptions of management. Jimmy Carter often became overly involved in the details of agency operations. He appeared to view his role in management somewhat like that of the commander of an atomic submarine. James Fallows, once chief speechwriter in the Carter White House, described Carter as a "perfectionist accustomed to thinking that to do the job right you must do it yourself."[4]

Lyndon Johnson, on the other hand, fell victim to the "single-solution syndrome." He had the idea that one professional group—economists—could operate a comprehensive policy and management control system for the government. This idea was embodied in Johnson's "programming, planning and budgeting system" (PPBS), announced with typical Johnsonian flourish to go into effect throughout the entire government on a single day, August 25, 1965. Both management concepts—Carter's view of the manager as a detail man and Johnson's economic-systems approach—require too detailed involvement on the part of the chief executive in administrative matters.

The most elaborate and developed concept of an administrative presidency strategy in the modern period was that of Richard Nixon. While the usual response to any mention of Nixon is to associate the entire period of his presidency with deviousness if not venality, a review of this history suggests that, considering his policy aims, Nixon was right to adopt an administrative presidency strategy for domestic affairs in his second term. One participant-observer, William Safire, predicted in 1975 "that one day the infiltration and reorganization which now seems so villainous will be carried out by more principled people under the banner of reform."[5]

Although Nixon was on the right track, true to form he proceeded in a heavy-handed way that might well have failed even without Watergate. Nixon's autobiography treats this subject in a way that reveals a hardness in his managerial philosophy:

> As much as it was within my power, I was determined during the second term to break the Eastern stranglehold on the executive branch and the federal govern-

[4]James Fallows, "The Passionless President," *The Atlantic Monthly*, May 1979, p. 38.

[5]William Safire, "Plots that Failed," *New York Times*, May 1, 1975. Safire was a presidential speech writer under Nixon, and later wrote a book on the Nixon administration, *Before the Fall: An Inside View of the Pre-Watergate White House* (New York: Belmont Tower Books, 1975).

ment. . . . I told Haldeman and Ehrlichman that I wanted an administration in-
fused with the spirit of the 1972 New Majority. I gave them four explicit criteria for
selection: loyalty, breadth, creativity—and moxie.[6]

Although it is still too early to judge, Ronald Reagan among recent presidents appears to have the best handle on the need for an administrative strategy. He has so far avoided the pitfalls of Nixon's heavy-handedness, Johnson's
grand design, and Carter's atomic-submarine approach to management. The
elements of Reagan's administrative approach are summarized in this final section, which considers the five main ingredients of an administrative presidency
strategy in reference to Reagan as well as other recent presidents. The five elements are: (1) selecting cabinet secretaries whose views are closely in line with
those of the president; (2) selecting subcabinet officials who also share the
president's values and objectives; (3) motivating cabinet and subcabinet officials to give attention to agency operations and administrative processes; (4)
using the budget process as the central organizing framework for public policymaking; and, finally, (5) avoiding over-reliance on centralized White House
clearance and control systems.

INGREDIENTS OF ADMINISTRATIVE PRESIDENCY

Cabinet Making

The experience of recent presidents suggests that the appointment of the right
people as cabinet members is fundamental to management control. The tempt-
ing and indeed customary approach to this task is to heal wounds and reach out
to many groups and constituencies in order to form a cabinet that is balanced
and broadly representative. *This healing process may be good for the soul, but
it is bad for the program.*

The literature of political science abounds with examples demonstrating
that adversarial relationships emerge between the president and members of his
cabinet. The balanced-cabinet approach exacerbates this situation. Nixon
came to this conclusion after three years, which is a long (but not unusually
long) learning period.

During his 1979 midterm shake-up, Carter fired four cabinet members, an
action that according to *U.S. News and World Report* was designed to "assert
more effective control and policy direction over the massive federal bureaucracy."[7] But, unfortunately for Carter, this purge was not deep enough to pro-

---

[6]Richard M. Nixon, *RN: The Memoirs of Richard Nixon*, vol. 2 (New York: Warner Books,
1978), p. 285.
   [7]*U.S. News and World Report*, July 30, 1979, p. 14.

duce a major change in his presidency. In this respect, Carter and Nixon were plagued by the same problems. It is very difficult to shift administrative strategy in the midst of an administration.

Reagan was fortunate in this regard. Many of the key planners of the Reagan presidency, notably E. Pendleton James, had learned the ropes under Nixon. They appreciated the importance of having cabinet officials philosophically in tune with the president. Edwin Meese and James set up a system to do this well before the election. Reagan chose cabinet officers whose experience and personality prepared them for a period of government service that above all would advance the purposes and program of his presidency.

The Appointment of Subcabinet Officials

A president's organizational strategy must deal not only with cabinet secretaries but also with the subcabinet. Again, Carter's experience is interesting. One reason that his midterm shake-up had limited impact was that it lacked depth. The Carter administration encompassed an incredible array of committed activists in subcabinet posts. Many of them had agendas of their own. Yet Carter's shake-up in 1979 applied only to four highly visible cabinet members felt to be marching to the wrong drummer—W. Michael Blumenthal (Treasury), Brock Adams (Transportation), Joseph Califano (Health, Education, and Welfare), and James Schlesinger (Energy). The layers below were relatively unaffected, and, indeed, could not have been massively restructured midstream, at least not without great difficulty. An article in the *National Journal* in 1978 quoted one assistant secretary as saying, "There is a belief that some assistant secretaries are in business for themselves. Officially, when they testify on the Hill, they say the right thing in respect to the president's budget and legislative program. But privately, they tell committee staff members, 'I don't really think that.' "[8]

Nixon learned this same lesson the hard way, but he had a better opportunity between terms to take steps to remedy the situation. Chapter 3 described Nixon's decision at the start of his first term to delegate to cabinet officers the responsibility for filling appointive positions in their agencies. In his autobiography eight years later, Nixon conceded the error of this decision. "I regretted that during the first term we had done a very poor job in the most basic business of every new administration of either party: We had failed to fill all key posts in the departments and agencies with people who were loyal to the presi-

[8]Dom Bonafede, "Carter Sounds Retreat from 'Cabinet' Government," *National Journal*, November 18, 1978, p. 1852. This article recounts an effort by the Carter White House to discipline subcabinet officials. Cabinet members were directed to make "personal and professional evaluations" of all presidential appointees. Two White House aides, Tim Kraft and Joel McCleary, were assigned to oversee these reviews, as well as new appointments for these positions.

dent and his programs.''[9] He went on to add a point of interpretation: ''Without this kind of leadership in the appointive positions, there is no way for the president to make any impact on the bureaucracy.''[10]

Nixon tried to rectify his mistake in his between-terms shake-up, which was far deeper and more systematic than Carter's. Nixon's shake-up reached beyond cabinet officers to hundreds of subcabinet and lower-level appointees. As the *National Journal* reported at the time, ''Loyalty to the president's programs was the crucial factor in the equation.''[11] Richard Neustadt characterized the 1973 Nixon shake-up as ''a determined effort to get control of the details and operations of the executive establishment.'' He noted that Nixon ''was not the first president who wanted to do this.''[12]

In his autobiography, Nixon is self-critical, describing the broadside call for cabinet, subcabinet, and White House staff resignations in 1973 as ''a mistake.'' ''I did not take into account the chilling effect this action would have on the morale of the people who had worked so hard during the election and who were naturally expecting a chance to savor the tremendous victory instead of suddenly having to worry about keeping their jobs.''[13]

The lesson is an obvious one, and it is the same point as that made above for cabinet officers. Once the horse is out of the barn, getting it back in, even at the start of a new term, is difficult and politically very expensive. Making the right appointments at the outset of a new government is one of the keys for a president in getting a managerial grip on the office.

Again, learning from the past, the Reagan administration picked its subcabinet carefully and took steps to tie them clearly and closely to the president. The Reagan strategy appears to be one of having his most doctrinaire supporters in these positions instead of in the more visible and exposed cabinet positions where they are more likely to be lightning rods for public criticism.

Motivating Political Officials

It is not enough to put the right people in the right positions. An administrative presidency strategy requires that steps be taken to motivate people in ways that involve the exercise of influence over the bureaucracy. The difficulties involved in doing this tend to be overstated. Washington is a city that lives by signals. The president does not need flow charts and elaborate administrative control systems. He can give signals in simple, but tremendously important, ways. Ex-

[9]Nixon, *Memoirs*, vol. 2, p. 284.
[10]*Ibid.*
[11]*National Journal*, March 13, 1973, p. 329.
[12]*Ibid.*
[13]Nixon, *Memoirs*, vol. 2, p. 285.

amples are invitations to state dinners, favorable mention at a press conference, rumors emanating from the White House that a particular appointee's actions are pleasing or displeasing, supportive phone calls, congratulatory notes, favorable budget decisions, invitations to meetings or the absence of same. These are the handles of official Washington. If used skillfully, they can reinforce the idea that presidential appointees should pursue presidential purposes and should devote time and attention to administrative processes.

A related aspect of an administrative approach to the presidency is *time*. The use of time by cabinet and subcabinet officials is little analyzed. But what research has been done indicates that the calendars of these officials tend to be dominated by matters and meetings external to their agency—congressional testimony, speeches outside of Washington, sessions with the press, maintaining contacts with interest groups, trips to China. For an administrative approach to the presidency to succeed, policy officials must spend more time at home in their agency—learning about programs and procedures and taking an active role in the work of their agency.

The relationship between political and career officials in internal agency activities is one of the hardest to establish and cannot be taken for granted. Frederick Malek, a prominent management official in the Nixon administration, stresses the need for direct, clear communication between political and career officials:

> Avoid middlemen or assistants as much as possible, particularly when assigning or reviewing work and reaching decisions. Deal directly with the bureau chief or responsible career officials so their own communications can be clearer down the line.[14]

Understanding and cooperation are also needed on the other side of this transaction. Dale McOmber, a veteran career official in the Office of Management and Budget, has written, "If the government is to work, there must be a symbiotic relationship between the policy official and civil servant. They need each other."[15] Frequently, federal bureaucrats cannot do what their policy chiefs want them to do simply because they do not know what it is. Not all bureaucrats are scheming crypto-members of the opposition devoted to undercutting presidential policies.

A second important timing consideration related to the behavior of cabinet and subcabinet officials concerns an official's tenure in office. The chief

[14]Frederick V. Malek, *Washington's Hidden Tragedy; The Failure to Make Government Work* (Glencoe, Ill.: The Free Press, 1978), p. 98.

[15]Dale McOmber, "An OMB Retrospect," *Public Budgeting and Finance,* Spring 1981, p. 83.

characteristic of the time horizon of many political officials is shortness. Two years is close to the average period in office for subcabinet officials. Three years is a long tour of duty. While there can be no easy rule of thumb, political officials should stay in office long enough to take advantage of having learned the ropes.

The Reagan administration took what to many observers was an inordinately long time to put its subcabinet in place. Hence, officials in the Reagan cabinet and subcabinet are likely to be in office further into the Reagan presidency than were their predecessors in other administrations, if for no other reason than the fact that they started later.

The Budget Process

There is an unfortunate tendency in government for political officials at the cabinet and subcabinet levels to rely on too many crosscutting decision systems. Officials who set up their office to have multiple decision systems with separate and relatively equal central staff groups make themselves an easy target for delay and obfuscatory tactics. While organizational strategies can differ, it is generally advisable to rely primarily on *one* primary organizing decision system in order to have decisions clearly understood and carried out. I believe the single best organizing system for government decision making and execution is the one that involves the clearest and most discrete unit of analysis—money. The budget process should be front and center.

Budgeting is a continuous process. It does not end with the transmittal of a budget to the Congress, or even its enactment. The budget process requires consistent and strong support by administration officials at many points in the process.

While this is not the place for a discourse on budgeting, the contrast between Reagan and Carter is instructive. In many ways the quite conservative Carter budgets of his last two years in office reflected the temper of the times, that is, the emerging national consensus about the need for spending reductions and restraint. The failure of the Carter administration to make more than modest spending cuts is a reflection of the lack of discipline and continuity in the critical processes of budget formulation, enactment, and execution. By contrast, the strong and creative use of the budget process by the Reagan administration has made budgeting the main instrument for both policymaking and management in Reagan's first two years in office. This will not always be the best organizational strategy. Nevertheless, the role of the budget process as a vehicle for policymaking and management in government is bound to be important as long as resources are scarce, and this is bound to be a long-term—even perpetual—condition.

The White House Staff

The fifth and final point about an administrative presidency strategy is a negative one. An administrative presidency must emanate from the president and crucially involves his relationship with his appointees in major executive branch agencies. For this relationship to be a successful one, it cannot be encumbered by a White House bureaucracy. This is a lesson Richard Nixon learned the hard way. At the start of his second term, Nixon dismantled his White House counter-bureaucracy and planned to rely instead on a smaller group of senior advisors. The idea was that these advisors and members of the cabinet would have opportunities for regular interaction with each other and with the president. The Nixon experience proves the truth of Robert Wood's admonition that as White House officials became more involved in details, the position and leverage of lower-level career agency officials are enhanced, rather than reduced. The penetration of political officials into administrative processes is not a job that can be done, or even supervised, from the White House. An administrative strategy requires delegation.

To conclude, I believe a managerial strategy is appropriate for the American presidency. Even if we assume that the president is successful in establishing a greater measure of managerial cohesion and control over the federal bureaucracy, there still exists an abundance of ways in which the president's power in this area and in others can be checked and balanced. It can be argued, in fact, that a managerial emphasis on the part of the president enhances popular control, given the tendency of industrialized states to become increasingly controlled from bureaucratic and technocratic power centers. The exercise of a greater measure of civilian control over the executive branch of the American national government, properly reflective of legal and constitutional requirements, is fully consistent with democratic values.

Documents

Documents

This section contains nine documents that help illuminate the strategies and issues considered in this volume. Following are brief descriptions of each of the documents selected.

1. *President Nixon's Television Address of August 8, 1969.* In this address to the nation, Nixon identified the main ideas of his "New Federalism" program and advanced four proposals—for welfare reform, revenue sharing, a new manpower training act, and the reorganization of the Office of Economic Opportunity. The speech was written by White House writer Raymond K. Price, Jr., who had a strong influence throughout the Nixon years in developing the positive themes of the Nixon administration's domestic program.[1]

2. *State of the Union Message, 1971.* The second most important statement of the Nixon administration's domestic program was the state of the union message of 1971. It was organized around what Nixon referred to as his "six great goals." Dissatisfied with the academic-sounding phrase "New Federalism," Nixon in this message tried out as an alternative the term "the New American Revolution."[2] The first of the six goals was welfare reform, a perennial issue of American domestic affairs. The others involved economic growth, the environment, health care, revenue sharing, and governmental reorganization.

3. *Executive Reorganization Message, March 25, 1971.* The third document is Nixon's 1971 message to the Congress on the reorganization of the executive branch. The plan was based on the work of the Advisory Council on Executive Organization, headed by Roy Ash. The council recommended the creation of four new superagencies to replace seven existing departments.

4. *Statement on Plans for the Second Term, November 27, 1972.* Although not as prominent as the preceding documents, the fourth is important as an early signal of plans for the administrative presidency strategy for the ill-fated Nixon second term. In remarks to the press in

---

[1]Presidential messages tend to reflect the orientation and point of view of their authors. Following the August 8 address, the president sent separate messages to the Congress on each of the four proposals the address contained. The revenue sharing message had a conservative cast and was written by Patrick J. Buchanan. The welfare message, on the other hand, was much more liberal and was written by William L. Safire. The two men were important White House writers and were influential in policy matters during the first term. Their work consistently differed in tone. Experienced hands could easily ascertain authorship.

[2]A year or so later, when it became clear that this new phrase had not caught on, it was dropped.

the helicopter hangar at Camp David just after his landslide reelection, Nixon explained why his cabinet was being reshuffled. "We are going to put greater responsibility on individual cabinet members for various functions that previously have been that of the White House staff." It was in this statement that Nixon said the White House staff had "grown like topsy" and would be the area of "the biggest cuts."

5. *Washington Star-News Interview.* Besides personnel and organizational changes for the second term, Nixon in a November 1972 interview with Garnett D. Horner of the *Washington Star-News* signaled major substantive changes. Expressing what Horner called "a puritan fervor he has seldom shown in public," Nixon flailed away at "the whole era of permisiveness," programs that "just threw money at problems," agencies that are "too fat, too bloated," and "the Georgetown cocktail set." When compared with the first four documents, the Horner interview shows the volatility of Nixon's ideas and feelings on domestic policy.

6. *1974 Article on Welfare Reform.* The next two documents are articles I wrote on welfare reform, one in 1974 and the second six years later as the Reagan administration got underway. They show the wide swing that took place in the 1970s on this issue. The first article, which appeared in the *Wall Street Journal*, argues that a comprehensive welfare reform plan on the order of a negative income tax or guaranteed income scheme is not the answer.

7. *1980 Article on Welfare Reform.* The second article on welfare reform was written for the journal *Commonsense*, published by the Republican National Committee. It deals with the very different setting of welfare policymaking on the eve of the 1980 presidential election. The argument here is that the block grants approach the Reagan administration favors is the wrong approach for reforming the nation's welfare programs.

8. *Inaugural Address, January 23, 1981.* Ronald Reagan's first statement of the policy aims of his administration was his inaugural address. It stressed the president's intention "to curb the size and influence of the Federal establishment," and reflects his federalism philosophy.

9. *State of the Union Message, 1982.* Ronald Reagan's state of the union message, delivered on January 26, 1982, concentrated on domestic affairs. He spelled out his "swap" and "turnback" plans, which included assigning to the states the responsibility for welfare and food stamps programs. Referring to swaps and turnbacks, Reagan said, "In a single stroke, we will be accomplishing a realignment that will end cumbersome administration and spiraling costs at the federal level."

Documents

Document 1

Television Address on the New Federalism

August 8, 1969

As you know, I returned last Sunday night from a trip around the world—a trip that took me to eight countries in nine days.

The purpose of this trip was to help lay the basis for a lasting peace, once the war in Vietnam is ended. In the course of it, I also saw once again the vigorous efforts so many new nations are making to leap the centuries into the modern world.

Every time I return to the United States after such a trip, I realize how fortunate we are to live in this rich land. We have the world's most advanced industrial economy, the greatest wealth ever known to man, the fullest measure of freedom ever enjoyed by any people, anywhere.

Yet we, too, have an urgent need to modernize our institutions—and our need is no less than theirs.

We face an urban crisis, a social crisis—and at the same time, a crisis of confidence in the capacity of government to do its job.

A third of a century of centralizing power and responsibility in Washington has produced a bureaucratic monstrosity, cumbersome, unresponsive, ineffective.

A third of a century of social experiment has left us a legacy of entrenched programs that have outlived their time or outgrown their purposes.

A third of a century of unprecedented growth and change has strained our institutions, and raised serious questions about whether they are still adequate to the times.

It is no accident, therefore, that we find increasing skepticism—not only among our young people, but among citizens everywhere—about the continuing capacity of government to master the challenges we face.

Nowhere has the failure of government been more tragically apparent than in its efforts to help the poor, especially in its system of public welfare.

Since taking office, one of my first priorities has been to repair the machinery of government, and to put it in shape for the 1970's. I have made many changes designed to improve the functioning of the Executive Branch. I have asked Congress for a number of important structural reforms; among others, a wide-ranging postal reform, a comprehensive reform of the draft, a reform of unemployment insurance, a reform of our hunger programs and reform of the present confusing hodge-podge of Federal grants-in-aid.

Last April 21, I sent Congress a message asking for a package of major tax reforms, including both the closing of loopholes and the removal of more than 2 million low-income families from the tax rolls altogether. I am glad Congress is now acting on tax reform, and I hope the Congress will begin to act on the other reforms that I have requested.

The purpose of all these reforms is to eliminate unfairness; to make government more effective as well as more efficient; and to bring an end to its chronic failure to deliver the service that it promises.

My purpose tonight, however, is not to review the past record, but to present a new set of reforms—a new set of proposals—a new and drastically different approach to the way in which government cares for those in need, and to the way the responsibilities are shared between the State and the Federal Government.

I have chosen to do so in a direct report to the people because these proposals call for public decisions of the first importance; because they represent a fundamental change in the nation's approach to one of its most pressing social problems; and because, quite deliberately, they also represent the first major reversal of the trend toward ever more centralization of government in Washington, D.C. After a third of a century of power flowing from the people and the States to Washington it is time for a New Federalism in which power, funds and responsibility will flow from Washington to the States and to the people.

During last year's election campaign, I often made a point that touched a responsive chord wherever I traveled.

I said that this nation became great not because of what government did for people, but because of what people did for themselves.

This new approach aims at helping the American people do more for themselves. It aims at getting everyone able to work off welfare rolls and onto payrolls.

It aims at ending the unfairness in a system that has become unfair to the welfare recipient, unfair to the working poor, and unfair to the taxpayer.

This new approach aims to make it possible for people—wherever in America they live—to receive their fair share of opportunity. It aims to ensure that people receiving aid, and who are able to work, contribute their fair share of productivity.

This new approach is embodied in a package of four measures: First, a complete replacement of the present welfare system; second, a comprehensive new job training and placement program; third, a revamping of the Office of Economic Opportunity; and fourth, a start on the sharing of Federal tax revenues with the States.

Next week—in three messages to the Congress and one statement—I will spell out in detail what these measures contain. Tonight I want to explain what they mean, what they are intended to achieve, and how they are related.

Whether measured by the anguish of the poor themselves, or by the drastically mounting burden on the taxpayer, the present welfare system has to be judged a colossal failure.

Our States and cities find themselves sinking in a Federal quagmire, as caseloads increase, as costs escalate, and as the welfare system stagnates enterprise and perpetuates dependency.

What began on a small scale in the depression 30's has become a huge monster in the prosperous 60's. And the tragedy is not only that it is bringing States and cities to the brink of financial disaster, but also that it is failing to meet the elementary human, social and financial needs of the poor.

It breaks up homes. It often penalizes work. It robs recipients of dignity. And it grows.

Benefit levels are grossly unequal—for a mother with three children, they range from an average of $263 a month in one State, down to an average of $39 in another State. Now such an inequality as this is wrong; no child is "worth" more in one State than in another State. One result of this inequality is to lure thousands more into already overcrowded inner cities, as unprepared for city life as they are for city jobs.

The present system creates an incentive for desertion. In most States a family is denied welfare payments if a father is present—even though he is unable to support his family. Now, in practice, this is what often happens: A father is unable (1) to find a job at all or (2) to find one that will support his children. So, to make the children eligible for welfare, he leaves home—and the children are denied the authority, the discipline and the love that come with having a father in the home. This is wrong.

The present system often makes it possible to receive more money on welfare than on a low-paying job. This creates an incentive not to work; and it also is unfair to the working poor. It is morally wrong for a family that is working to try to make ends meet to receive less than the family across the street on welfare. This has been bitterly resented by the man who works, and rightly so—the rewards are just the opposite of what they should be. Its effect is to draw people off payrolls and onto welfare rolls—just the opposite of what Government should be doing. To put it bluntly and simply—any system which makes it more profitable for a man not to work than to work, or which encourages a man to desert his family rather than to stay with his family, is wrong and indefensible.

We cannot simply ignore the failures of welfare, or expect them to go away. In the past eight years, three million more people have been added to the welfare rolls—and this in a period of low unemployment. If the present trend continues, another four million will join the welfare rolls by 1975. The financial cost will be crushing; and the human cost will be suffocating.

That is why tonight I, therefore, propose that we will abolish the present welfare system and that we adopt in its place a new family assistance system. Initially, this new system will cost more than welfare. But unlike welfare, it is designed to correct the condition it deals with and, thus, to lessen the long-range burden and cost.

Under this plan, the so-called "adult categories" of aid—aid to the aged, the blind and disabled—would be continued and a national minimum standard for benefits would be set, with the Federal Government contributing to its cost and also sharing the cost of additional State payments above that amount.

But the program now called "Aid to Families with Dependent Children"—the program we all normally think of when we think of "welfare"—would be done away with completely. The new family assistance system I propose in its place rests essentially on these three principles: Equality of treatment across the nation, a work requirement and a work incentive.

Its benefits would go to the working poor as well as the non-working; to families with dependent children headed by a father, as well as to those headed by a mother; and a basic Federal minimum would be provided, the same in every State.

What I am proposing is that the Federal Government build a foundation under the income of every American family with dependent children that cannot care for itself—wherever in America that family may live.

For a family of four now on welfare, with no outside income, the basic Federal payment would be $1,600 a year. States could add to that amount and most States would add to it. In no case would anyone's present level of benefits be lowered.

At the same time, this foundation would be one on which the family itself could build. Outside earnings would be encouraged, not discouraged. The new worker could keep the first $60 a month of outside earnings with no reduction in his benefits; then beyond that, his benefits would be reduced by only 50 cents for each dollar earned.

By the same token, a family head already employed at low wages could get a family assistance supplement; those who work would no longer be discriminated against. For example, a family of five in which the father earns $2,000 a year—which is the hard fact of life for many families in America today—would get family assistance payments of $1,260, so that they would have a total income of $3,260. A family of seven earning $3,000 a year would have its income raised to $4,360.

Thus, for the first time, the government would recognize that it has no less an obligation to the working poor than to the non-working poor; and for the first time, benefits would be scaled in such a way that it would always pay to work.

With such incentives, most recipients who can work will want to work. This is part of the American character.

But what of the others—those who can work but choose not to?

The answer is very simple.

Under this proposal, everyone who accepts benefits must also accept work or training provided suitable jobs are available either locally or at some distance if transportation is provided. The only exceptions would be those unable to work and mothers of pre-school children.

Even mothers of pre-school children, however, would have the opportunity to work—because I am also proposing along with this a major expansion of day-care centers to make it possible for mothers to take jobs by which they can support themselves and their children.

This national floor under incomes for working or dependent families is not a "guaranteed income." Under the guaranteed income proposal, everyone would be assured a minimum income, regardless of how much he was capable of earning, regardless of what his need was, regardless of whether or not he was willing to work.

During the Presidential campaign last year, I opposed such a plan. I oppose it now and I will continue to oppose it, for this reason: A guaranteed income would undermine the incentive to work; the family assistance plan that I propose increases the incentive to work.

A guaranteed income establishes a right without any responsibilities; family assistance recognizes a need and establishes a responsibility. It provides help to those in need, and in turn, requires that those who receive help work to the extent of their capabilities. There is no reason why one person should be taxed so that another can choose to live idly.

In States that now have benefit levels above the Federal floor, family assistance would help ease the State's financial burdens. But in 20 States—those in which poverty is most widespread—the new Federal floor would be above present average benefits and would mean a leap upward for many thousands of families that cannot care for themselves.

Now I would like to turn to the job training proposals that are part of our full opportunity concept. America prides itself on being the "land of opportunity." I deeply believe in this ideal, as I am sure everyone listening to me also believes in this ideal.

Full opportunity means the chance for upward mobility on every rung of the economic ladder—for every American, no matter what the handicaps of birth.

The cold, hard truth is that a child born to a poor family has far less chance to make a good living than a child born to a middle-income family.

He is born poor, fed poorly; and if his family is on welfare, he starts life in an atmosphere of handout and dependency; often he receives little preparation for work and less inspiration. The wonder of the American character is that so many have the spark and the drive to fight their way up. But for millions of others, the burden of poverty in early life snuffs out that spark.

The new family assistance would provide aid for needy families; it would establish a work requirement and a work incentive; but these in turn require effective programs of job training and job placement—including a chance to qualify not just for any jobs, but for good jobs, that provide both additional self-respect and full self-support.

Therefore, I am also sending a message to Congress calling for a complete overhaul of the nation's manpower training services.

The Federal Government's job training programs have been a terrible tangle of confusion and waste.

To remedy the confusion, arbitrariness and rigidity of the present system, the new manpower training act would basically do three things. It would pull together the jumble of programs that presently exist, and equalize standards of eligibility.

It would provide flexible funding—so that Federal money would follow the demands of labor and industry and flow into those programs that people most want and most need.

It would decentralize administration, gradually moving it away from the Washington bureaucracy and turning it over to States and localities.

In terms of its symbolic importance, I can hardly overemphasize this last point. For the first time, applying the principles of the New Federalism, administration of a major established Federal program would be turned over to the States and local governments, recognizing that they are in a position to do the job better.

For years, thoughtful Americans have talked of the need to decentralize government. The time has come to begin.

Federal job training programs have grown to vast proportions, costing more than a billion dollars a year. Yet they are essentially local in character. As long as the Federal Government continues to bear the cost, they can perfectly well be run by States and local governments, and that way they can be better adapted to specific State and local needs.

The Manpower Training Act will have other provisions specifically designed to help move people off welfare rolls and onto payrolls.

A computerized job bank would be established, to match job seekers with job vacancies.

For those on welfare, a $30 a month bonus would be offered as an incentive to go into job training.

For heads of families now on welfare, 150,000 new training slots would be opened.

As I mentioned previously, greatly expanded day-care facilities would be provided for the children of welfare mothers who choose to work. However, these would be day-care centers with a difference. There is no single ideal to which this Administration is more firmly committed than to the enriching of a child's first five years of life, and, thus, helping lift the poor out of misery at a time when a lift can help the most. Therefore, these day-care centers would offer more than custodial care; they would also be devoted to the development of vigorous young minds and bodies. As a further dividend, the day-care centers would offer employment to many welfare mothers themselves.

One common theme running through my proposals tonight is that of providing full opportunity for every American. A second theme is that of trying to equip every American to play a productive role and a third is that of reshaping, reforming, and innovating the Government itself to make it workable.

The Office of Economic Opportunity is basically an innovative agency— and thus it has a vital place in our efforts to develop new programs and apply new knowledge. But in order to do effectively what it can do best, OEO itself needs reorganization.

This Administration has completed a thorough study of OEO. We have assigned it a leading role in the effort to develop and test new approaches to the solving of social problems. OEO is to be a laboratory agency where new ideas for helping people are tried on a pilot basis. When they prove successful, they can be spun off to operating departments or agencies—just as the space agency, for example, spun off the weather satellite and the communications satellite when these proved successful—then OEO would be free to concentrate on breaking even newer ground.

The new OEO organization to be announced next week will stress this role. It also will stress accountability, a clear separation of functions, and a tighter, more effective organization of field operations.

We come now to a proposal which I consider profoundly important to the future of our Federal system of shared responsibilities since, when we speak of poverty or jobs, or opportunity or making government more effective or getting it closer to the people, it bears directly on the financial plight of our States and cities.

We can no longer have effective government at any level unless we have it at all levels. There is too much to be done for the cities to do it alone, or for Washington to do it alone, or for the States to do it alone.

For a third of a century, power and responsibility have flowed toward Washington—and Washington has taken for its own the best sources of revenue.

We intend to reverse this tide, and to turn back to the States a greater measure of responsibility—not as a way of avoiding problems, but as a better way of solving problems.

Along with this would go a share of Federal revenues. I shall propose to the Congress next week that a set portion of the revenues, from Federal income taxes be remitted directly to the States—with a minimum of Federal restrictions on how those dollars are to be used, and with a requirement that a percentage of them be channeled through for the use of local governments.

The funds provided under this program will not be great in the first year. But the principle will have been established, and the amounts will increase as our budgetary situation improves.

This start on revenue sharing is a step toward what I call the New Federalism. It is a gesture of faith in America's State and local governments and in the principle of democratic self-government.

With this revenue sharing proposal we follow through on the commitment I made in the last campaign. We follow through on a mandate which the electorate gave us last November.

In recent years, we all have concentrated a great deal of attention on what we commonly call the "crisis of the cities." These proposals I have made are addressed in part to that, but they also are focused much more broadly.

They are addressed to the crisis of government—to adapting its structures and making it manageable.

They are addressed to the crisis of poverty and need—which is rural as well as urban. This Administration is committed to full opportunity on the farm as well as in the city; to a better life for rural America; to ensuring that government is responsive to the needs of rural America as well as urban America. These proposals will advance these goals.

I have discussed these four matters together because they make both a package and a pattern. They should be studied together, debated together and seen in perspective.

Now these proposals will be controversial, just as any new program is controversial. They also are expensive. Let us face that fact frankly and directly.

The first-year costs of the new family assistance program, including the child care centers and job training, would be $4 billion. I deliberated long and hard over whether we could afford such an outlay. I decided in favor of it for two reasons: First, because the costs would not begin until fiscal 1971, when I expect the funds to be available within the budget; and second, because I concluded that this is a reform we cannot afford not to undertake. The cost of continuing the present system, in financial as well as human terms, is staggering if projected into the 1970's.

Revenue sharing would begin in the middle of fiscal 1971, at a half-year cost of a half billion dollars. This cuts into the Federal budget, but it represents relief for the equally hard-pressed States. It would help curb the rise in State and local taxes which are such a burden to millions of American families.

Overall, we would be spending more—in the short run—to help people who now are poor and who now are unready for work or unable to find work.

But I see it this way: Every businessman, every working man knows what "start-up costs" are. They are heavy investments made in early years in the expectation that they will more than pay for themselves in future years.

The investment in these proposals is a human investment; it also is a "start-up cost" in turning around our dangerous decline into welfarism in America. We cannot produce productive people with the antiquated, wheezing, overloaded machine we now call the welfare system.

If we fail to make this investment in work incentives now, if we merely try to patch up the system here and there, we will only be pouring good money after bad in ever-increasing amounts.

If we do invest in this modernization, the heavy-burdened taxpayer at least will have the chance to see the end of the tunnel. And the man who only looks ahead to a lifetime of dependency will see hope—hope for a life of work and pride and dignity.

In the final analysis, we cannot talk our way out of poverty; we cannot legislate our way out of poverty, but this Nation can work its way out of poverty. What America needs now is not more welfare, but more "workfare."

The task of this government, the great task of our people, is to provide the training for work, the incentive for work, the opportunity for work, and the reward for work. Together these measures are a first long step in this direction.

For those in the welfare system today who are struggling to fight their way out of poverty, these measures offer a way to independence through the dignity of work.

For those able to work these measures provide new opportunities to learn work, and to find work.

For the working poor—the forgotten poor—these measures offer a fair share in the assistance given to the poor.

This new system establishes a direct link between the government's willingness to help the needy and the willingness of the needy to help themselves.

It removes the present incentive not to work, and substitutes an incentive to work; it removes the present incentive for families to break apart, and substitutes an incentive for families to stay together.

It removes the blatant inequities, injustices and indignities of the welfare system.

It establishes a basic Federal floor so that children in any State can have at least the minimum essentials of life.

Together, these measures cushion the impact of welfare costs on States and localities, many of which have found themselves in fiscal crisis as costs have spiraled.

They bring reason, order and purpose into a tangle of overlapping programs, and show that Government can be made to work.

Poverty will not be defeated by a stroke of a pen signing a check; and it will not be reduced to nothing overnight with slogans or ringing exhortations.

Poverty is not only a state of income. It is also a state of mind and a state of health. Poverty, must be conquered without sacrificing the will to work, for if we take the route of the permanent handout, the American character will itself be impoverished.

In my recent trip around the world, I visited countries in all stages of economic development; countries with different social systems, different economic systems, different political systems.

In all of them, however, I found that one event caught the imagination of the people and lifted their spirits almost beyond measure: The trip of APOLLO to the moon and back. On that historic day, when the astronauts set foot on the moon, the spirit of APOLLO truly swept through this world—it was a spirit of peace and brotherhood and adventure, a spirit that thrilled to the knowledge that man had dreamed the impossible, dared the impossible, and done the impossible.

Abolishing poverty, putting an end to dependency—like reaching the moon a generation ago, may seem to be impossible, But in the spirit of APOLLO, we can lift our sights and marshal our best efforts. We can resolve to make this the year, not that we reached the goal, but that we turned the corner; turned the corner from a dismal cycle of dependency toward a new birth of independence; from despair toward hope; from an ominously mounting impotence of government to a new effectiveness of government, and toward a full opportunity for every American to share the bounty of this rich land.

Document 2

State of the Union Address of the President of the United States

Delivered before a joint session of the Senate and the House of Representatives, January 22, 1971

Mr. Speaker, Mr. President, My Colleagues in the Congress, Our Distinguished Guests, My Fellow Americans:

As this 92nd Congress begins its session, America has lost a great Senator, and all of us who had the privilege to know him have lost a loyal friend. I had the privilege of visiting Senator Russell in the hospital just a few days before he died. He never spoke about himself. He only spoke eloquently about the need for a strong national defense.

In tribute to one of the most magnificent Americans of all time, I respectfully ask that all those here rise in silent prayer for Senator Russell.

[All present rose in silent prayer.]

Thank you.

Mr. Speaker, before I begin my formal address, I want to use this opportunity to congratulate all of those who were winners in the rather spirited contest for leadership positions in the House and the Senate, and also to express my condolences to the losers. I know how both of you feel. I particularly want to join with all the Members of the House and the Senate as well in congratulating the new Speaker of the United States Congress. And to those new Members of the House who may have some doubts about the possibilities for advancement in the years ahead, I would remind you that the Speaker and I met just twenty four years ago in this chamber as freshmen Members of the 86th Congress. As you see, we have both come up in the world a bit since that time.

This 92nd Congress has a chance to be recorded as the greatest Congress in America's history.

In these troubled years just past, America has been going through a long nightmare of war and division, of crime and inflation. Even more deeply, we have gone through a long, dark night of the American spirit. But now that night is ending. Now we must let our spirits soar again. Now we are ready for the lift of a driving dream.

The people of this nation are eager to get on with the quest for new greatness. They see challenges, and they are prepared to meet those challenges. It is for us here to open the doors that will set free again the real greatness of this nation—the genius of the American people.

How shall we meet this challenge? How can we truly open the doors, and set free the full genius of our people?

The way in which the 92nd Congress answers these questions will determine its place in history. But more importantly, it can determine this nation's place in history as we enter the third century of our independence.

Tonight, I shall present to the Congress six great goals. I shall ask not simply for more new programs in the old framework, but to change the framework itself—to reform the entire structure of American government so we can make it again fully responsive to the needs and the wishes of the American people.

If we act boldly—if we seize this moment and achieve these goals—we can close the gap between promise and performance in American government, and bring together the resources of the nation and the spirit of the people.

In discussing these great goals, I am dealing tonight only with matters on the domestic side of the nation's agenda. I shall make a separate report to the Congress and the nation next month on developments in our foreign policy.

The first of these six great goals is already before the Congress.

I urge that the unfinished business of the 91st Congress be made the first priority business of the 92nd.

Over the next two weeks, I will call upon Congress to take action on more than 35 pieces of proposed legislation on which action was not completed last year.

The most important is welfare reform.

The present welfare system has become a monstrous, consuming outrage—an outrage against the community, against the taxpayer, and particularly against the children it is supposed to help.

We may honestly disagree, as we do, on what to do about it. But we can all agree that we must meet the challenge not by pouring more money into a bad program, but by abolishing the present welfare system and adopting a new one.

So let us place a floor under the income of every family with children in America—and without those demeaning, soul-stifling affronts to human dignity that so blight the lives of welfare children today. But let us also establish an effective work incentive and an effective work requirement.

Let us provide the means by which more can help themselves. This shall be our goal. Let us generously help those who are not able to help themselves. But let us stop helping those who are able to help themselves but refuse to do so.

The second great goal is to achieve what Americans have not enjoyed since 1957—full prosperity in peacetime.

The tide of inflation has turned. The rise in the cost of living, which had been gathering dangerous momentum in the late Sixties, was reduced last year. Inflation will be further reduced this year.

But as we have moved from runaway inflation toward reasonable price stability, and at the same time as we have been moving from a wartime economy to a peacetime economy, we have paid a price in increased unemployment.

We should take no comfort from the fact that the level of unemployment in this transition from a wartime to a peacetime economy is lower than any peacetime year of the 1960s.

This is not good enough for the man who is unemployed in the Seventies. We must do better for workers in peacetime and we will do better.

To achieve this, I will submit an expansionary budget this year—one that will help stimulate the economy and thereby open up new job opportunities for millions of Americans.

It will be a full employment budget, a budget designed to be in balance if the economy were operating at its peak potential. By spending as if we were at full employment, we will help to bring about full employment.

I ask the Congress to accept these expansionary policies—to accept the concept of the full employment budget.

At the same time, I ask the Congress to cooperate in resisting expenditures that go beyond the limits of the full employment budget. For as we wage a campaign to bring about a widely shared prosperity, we must not re-ignite the fires of inflation and so undermine that prosperity.

With the stimulus and the discipline of a full employment budget; with the commitment of the independent Federal Reserve System to provide fully for the monetary needs of a growing economy; and with a much greater effort on the part of labor and management to make their wage and price decisions in the light of the national interest and their own long-run best interests—then for the worker, the farmer, the consumer, and for Americans everywhere we shall gain the goal of a new prosperity; more jobs, more income and more profits, without inflation and without war.

This is a great goal, and one that we can achieve together.

The third great goal is to continue the effort so dramatically begun last year: to restore and enhance our natural environment.

Building on the foundation laid in the 37-point program I submitted to Congress last year, I will propose a strong new set of initiatives to clean up our air and water, to combat noise, and to preserve and restore our surroundings.

I will propose programs to make better use of our land, and to encourage a balanced national growth—growth that will revitalize our rural heartland and enhance the quality of life throughout America.

And not only to meet today's needs but to anticipate those of tomorrow, I will put forward the most extensive program every proposed by a President of the United States to expand the nation's parks, recreation areas and open spaces in a way that truly brings parks to the people, where the people are. For only if we leave a legacy of parks will the next generation have parks to enjoy.

As a fourth great goal, I will offer a far-reaching set of proposals for improving America's health care and making it available more fairly to more people.

I will propose:

A program to insure that no American family will be prevented from obtaining basic medical care by inability to pay.

A major increase in and redirection of aid to medical schools, to greatly increase the number of doctors and other health personnel.

Incentives to improve the delivery of health services, to get more medical care resources into those areas that have not been adequately served, to make greater use of medical assistants and to slow the alarming rise in the costs of medical care.

New programs to encourage better preventive medicine, by attacking the causes of disease and injury, and by providing incentives to doctors to keep people well rather than just to treat them when they are sick.

I will also ask for an appropriation of an extra $100 million to launch an intensive campaign to find a cure for cancer, and I will ask later for whatever additional funds can effectively be used. The time has come in America when the same kind of concentrated effort that split the atom and took man to the moon should be turned toward conquering this dread disease. Let us make a total national commitment to achieve this goal.

America has long been the wealthiest nation in the world. Now it is time we became the healthiest nation in the world.

The fifth great goal is to strengthen and to renew our State and local governments.

As we approach our 200th anniversary in 1976, we remember that this Nation launched itself as a loose confederation of separate States, without a workable central government. At that time, the mark of its leaders' vision was that they quickly saw the need to balance the separate powers of the States with a government of central powers.

And so they gave us a Constitution of balanced powers, of unity with diversity—and so clear was their vision that it survives today as the oldest written Constitution still in force in the world today.

For almost two centuries since—and dramatically in the 1930s—at those great turning points when the question has been between the States and the

Federal Government, that question has been resolved in favor of a stronger central and Federal Government.

During this time the Nation grew and the Nation prospered. But one thing history tells us is that no great movement goes in the same direction forever. Nations change, they adapt, or they slowly die.

The time has now come in America to reverse the flow of power and resources from the States and communities to Washington, and start power and resources flowing back from Washington to the States and communities and, more important, to the people, all across America.

The time has come for a new partnership between the Federal Government and the States and localities—a partnership in which we entrust the States and localities with a larger share of the Nation's responsibilities, and in which we share our Federal revenues with them so they can meet those responsibilities.

To achieve this goal, I propose to the Congress tonight that we enact *a plan of revenue sharing*, historic in scope, and bold in concept.

All across America today, States and cities are confronted with a financial crisis. Some already have been cutting back on essential services—for example, just recently San Diego and Cleveland cut back on trash collections. Most are caught between the prospects of bankruptcy on the one hand and adding to an already crushing tax burden on the other.

As one indication of the rising costs of local government, I discovered the other day that my hometown of Whittier, California, which has a population of only 67,000, has a larger budget for 1971 than the entire Federal budget was in 1791.

Now the time has come to take a new direction, and once again to introduce a new and more creative balance in our approach to government.

So let us put the money where the needs are. And let us put the power to spend it where the people are.

I propose that the Congress make a $16 billion investment in renewing State and local government. $5 billion of this will be in new and unrestricted funds, to be used as the States and localities see fit. The other $11 billion will be provided by allocating $1 billion of new funds and converting one-third of the money going to the present narrow-purpose aid programs into Federal revenue sharing funds for six broad purposes—for urban development, rural development, education, transportation, job training and law enforcement—but with the States and localities making their own local decisions on how it should be spent within each category.

For the next fiscal year, this would increase total Federal aid to the States and localities by more than 25 percent over the present level.

The revenue sharing proposals I send to the Congress will include the safeguards against discrimination that accompany all other Federal funds allocated to the States. Neither the President nor the Congress nor the conscience of the Nation can permit money which comes from all the people to be used in a way which discriminates against some of the people.

The Federal Government will still have a large and vital role to play in achieving our national purposes. Established functions that are clearly and essentially Federal in nature will still be performed by the Federal Government. New functions that need to be sponsored or performed by the Federal Government—such as those I have urged tonight in welfare and health—will be added to the Federal agenda. Whenever it makes the best sense for us to act as a whole nation, the Federal Government should and will lead the way. But where State or local governments can better do what needs to be done, let us see that they have the resources to do it there.

Under this plan, the Federal Government will provide the States and localities with more money and less interference—and by cutting down the interference the same amount of money will go a lot further.

Let us share our resources:

Let us share them to rescue the States and localities from the brink of financial crisis. Let us share them to give homeowners and wage earners a chance to escape from ever-higher property taxes and sales taxes.

Let us share our resources for two other reasons as well.

The first of these reasons has to do with government itself, and the second has to do with each of us, with the individual.

Let's face it. Most Americans today are simply fed up with government at all levels. They will not—and should not—continue to tolerate the gap between promise and performance in Government.

The fact is that we have made the Federal Government so strong it grows muscle-bound and the States and localities so weak they approach impotence.

If we put more power in more places, we can make government more creative in more places. That way we multiply the number of people with the ability to make things happen—and we can open the way to a new burst of creative energy throughout America.

The final reason I urge this historic shift is much more personal, for each and for every one of us.

As everything seems to have grown bigger, and more complex in America; as the forces that shape our lives seem to have grown more distant and more impersonal a great feeling of frustration has crept across this land.

Whether it is the working man who feels neglected, the black man who feels oppressed or the mother concerned about her children, there has been a growing feeling that "things are in the saddle, and ride mankind."

Millions of frustrated young Americans today are crying out—asking not what will government do for me, but what can I do, how can I contribute, how can I matter?

So let us answer them. Let us say to them and let us say to all Americans: "We hear you and we will give you a chance. We are going to give you a new chance to have more to say about the decisions that affect your future—a chance to participate in government—because we are going to provide more centers of power where what you can do can make a difference that you can see and feel in you own life and the life of your whole community."

The further away government is from people, the stronger government becomes and the weaker people become. And a nation with a strong government and a weak people is an empty shell.

I reject the patronizing idea that government in Washington, D.C. is inevitably more wise, more honest and more efficient than government at the local or State level. The honesty and efficiency of government depends on people. Government at all levels has good people and bad people. And the way to get more good people into government is to give them more opportunity to do good things.

The idea that a bureaucratic elite in Washington knows best what is best for people everywhere and that you cannot trust local government is really a contention that you cannot trust people to govern themselves. This notion is completely foreign to the American experience. Local government is the government closest to the people and it is more responsive to the individual person; it is people's government in a far more intimate way than the government in Washington can ever be.

People came to America because they wanted to determine their own future rather than to live in a country where others determined their future for them.

What this change means is that once again in America we are placing our trust in people.

I have faith in people. I trust the judgment of people. Let us give the people of America a chance, a bigger voice in deciding for themselves those questions that so greatly affect their lives.

The sixth great goal is a complete reform of the Federal Government itself.

Based on a long and intensive study with the aid of the best advice obtainable, I have concluded that a sweeping reorganization of the Executive Branch is needed if the government is to keep up with the times and with the needs of the people.

I propose therefore that we reduce the present twelve Cabinet Departments to eight.

I propose that the Departments of State, Treasury, Defense and Justice remain, but that all the other departments be consolidated into four: Human Resources, Community Development, Natural Resources, and Economic Development.

Let us look at what these would be:

First, a department dealing with the concerns of people—as individuals, as members of a family—a department focused on human needs.

Second, a department concerned with the community—rural communities and urban—and with all that it takes to make a community function as a community.

Third, a department concerned with our physical environment, and with the preservation and balanced use of those great natural resources on which our nation depends.

An fourth, a department concerned with our prosperity—with our jobs, our businesses, and those many activities that keep our economy running smoothly and well.

Under this plan, rather than dividing up our departments by narrow subject, we would organize them around the great purposes of government. Rather than scattering responsibility by adding new levels of bureaucracy, we would focus and concentrate the responsibility for getting problems solved.

With these four departments, when we have a problem we will know where to go—and the department will have the authority and the resources to do something about it.

Over the years we have added departments and created agencies at the Federal level, each to serve a new constituency or to handle a particular task—and these have grown and multiplied in what has become a hopeless confusion of form and function.

The time has come to match our structure to our purposes—to look with a fresh eye, and to organize the government by conscious, comprehensive design to meet the new needs of a new era.

One hundred years ago, Abraham Lincoln stood on a battlefield and spoke of a government of the people, by the people, and for the people. Too often since then, we have become a nation of the Government, by the Government, and for the Government.

By enacting these reforms, we can renew that principle that Lincoln stated so simply and so well.

By giving everyone's voice a chance to be heard, we will have government that truly is of the people.

By creating more centers of meaningful power, more places where decisions that really count can be made, by giving more people a chance to do something, we can have government that truly is by the people.

And by setting up a completely modern, functional system of government at the national level, we in Washington will at last be able to provide government that truly is for the people.

I realize that what I am asking is that not only the Executive Branch in Washington but even this Congress will have to change by giving up some of its power.

Change is hard. But without change there can be no progress. And for each of us the question then becomes, not "Will change cause me inconvenience?" but "Will change bring the country progress for America?"

Giving up power is hard. But I would urge all of you, as leaders of this country, to remember that the truly revered leaders in world history are those who gave power to people, not those who took it away.

As we consider these reforms we will be acting, not for the next ten years, but for the next hundred years.

So let us approach these six great goals with a sense, not only of this moment in history, but also of history itself.

Let us act with the willingness to work together and the vision and the boldness and the courage of those great Americans who met in Philadelphia almost 190 years ago to write a Constitution.

Let us leave a heritage as they did—not just for our children but for millions yet unborn—of a nation where every American will have a chance not only to live in peace and enjoy prosperity and opportunity, but to participate in a system of government where he knows not only his votes but his ideas count—a system of government which will provide the means for America to reach heights of achievement undreamed of before.

Those men who met in Philadelphia left a great heritage because they had a vision—not only of what the nation was, but of what it could become.

As I think of that vision, I recall that America was founded as the land of the open door—as a haven for the oppressed, a land of opportunity, a place of refuge and of hope.

When the first settlers opened the door of America three and a half centuries ago, they came to escape persecution and to find opportunity—and they left wide the door of welcome for others to follow.

When the thirteen colonies declared their independence almost two centuries ago, they opened the door to a new vision of liberty and of human fulfillment—not just for an elite, but for all.

To the generations that followed, America's was the open door that beckoned millions from the old world to the new in search of a better life, a freer life, a fuller life, in which by their own decisions they could shape their own destinies.

For the black American, the Indian, the Mexican-American, and for those others in our land who have not had an equal chance, the nation at last has begun to confront the need to press open the door of full and equal opportunity, and of human dignity.

For all Americans, with these changes I have proposed tonight we can open the door to a new era of opportunity. We can open the door in full and effective participation in the decisions that affect their lives. We can open the door to a new partnership among governments at all levels, and between those governments and the people themselves. And by so doing, we can open wide the doors of human fulfillment for millions of people here in America now and in the years to come.

In the next few weeks I will spell out in greater detail the way I propose that we achieve these six great goals. I ask this Congress to be responsive. If it is, then the 92nd Congress—your Congress, our Congress—at the end of its term, will be able to look back on a record more splendid than any in our history.

This can be the Congress that helped us end the longest war in the nation's history, and end it in a way that will give us at last a genuine chance to enjoy what we have not had in this century—a full generation of peace.

This can be the Congress that helped achieve an expanding economy, with full employment and without inflation—and without the deadly stimulus of war.

This can be the Congress that reformed a welfare system that has robbed recipients of their dignity while it robbed States and cities of their resources.

This can be the Congress that pressed forward the rescue of our environment, and established for the next generation an enduring legacy of parks for the people.

This can be the Congress that launched a new era in American medicine, in which the quality of medical care was enhanced while the costs were made less burdensome.

But above all, what this Congress can be remembered for is opening the way to a New American Revolution—a peaceful revolution in which power was turned back to the people—in which government at all levels was refreshed and renewed, and made truly responsive. This can be a revolution as profound, as far reaching, as exciting, as that first revolution almost 200 years ago—and it can mean that just five years from now America will enter its third century as a young nation new in spirit, with all the vigor and freshness with which it began its first century.

My colleagues in the Congress, these are great goals, and they can make the sessions of this Congress a great moment for America. So let us pledge together to go forward together—by achieving these goals to give America the foundation today for a new greatness tomorrow and in all the years to come—and in so doing to make this the greatest Congress in the history of this great and good country.

Message on Executive Reorganization

The President's Message to the Congress Proposing the Establishment of a Department of Natural Resources, Department of Community Development, Department of Human Resources, and Department of Economic Affairs. March 25, 1971

To the Congress of the United States:

When I suggested in my State of the Union Message that "most Americans today are simply fed up with government at all levels," there was some surprise that such a sweeping indictment of government would come from within the government itself. Yet it is precisely there, within the government itself, that frustration with government is often most deeply experienced.

A President and his associates often feel that frustration as they try to fulfill their promises to the people. Legislators feel that frustration as they work to carry out the hopes of their constituents. And dedicated civil servants feel that frustration as they strive to achieve in action the goals which have been established in law.

GOOD MEN AND BAD MECHANISMS

The problem with government is not, by and large, the people in government. It is a popular thing, to be sure, for the public to blame elected officials and for elected officials to blame appointed officials when government fails to perform. There are times when such criticism is clearly justified. But after a quarter century of observing government from a variety of vantage points, I have concluded that the people who work in government are more often the victims than the villains when government breaks down. Their spirit has usually been willing. It is the structure that has been weak.

Good people cannot do good things with bad mechanisms. But bad mechanisms can frustrate even the noblest aims. That is why so many public servants—of both political parties, of high rank and low, in both the legislative and executive branches—are often disenchanted with government these days. That is also why so many voters feel that the results of elections make remarkably little difference in their lives.

Just as inadequate organization can frustrate good men and women, so it can dissipate good money. At the Federal level alone we have spent some $1.1 trillion on domestic programs over the last 25 years, but we have not realized a fair return on this investment. The more we spend, the more it seems we need to spend and while our tax bills are getting bigger our problems are getting worse.

No, the major cause of the ineffectiveness of government is not a matter of men or of money. It is principally a matter of machinery. It will do us little good to change personnel or to provide more resources unless we are willing to undertake a critical review of government's overall design.

Most people do not pay much attention to mechanical questions. What happens under the hood of their automobile, for example, is something they leave to the specialists at the garage. What they do care about, however, is how well the automobile performs. Similarly, most people are willing to leave the mechanical questions of government organization to those who have specialized in that subject—and to their elected leaders. But they do care very deeply about how well the government performs.

At this moment in our history, most Americans have concluded that government is not performing well. It promises much, but it does not deliver what it promises. The great danger, in my judgment, is that this momentary disillusionment with government will turn into a more profound and lasting loss of faith.

We must fight that danger. We must restore the confidence of the people in the capacities of their government. In my view, that obligation now requires us to give more profound and more critical attention to the question of government organization than any single group of American leaders has done since the Constitutional Convention adjourned in Philadelphia in September of 1787. As we strive to bring about a new American Revolution, we must recognize that central truth which those who led the original American Revolution so clearly understood: often it is *how* the government is put together that determines how *well* the government can do its job.

This is not a partisan matter, for there is no Republican way and no Democratic way to reorganize the government. This is not a matter for dogmatic dispute, for there is no single, ideal blueprint which will immediately bring good order to Federal affairs. Nor is this a matter to be dealt with once and then forgotten. For it is important that our political institutions remain constantly responsive to changing times and changing problems.

RENEWED INTEREST IN COMPREHENSIVE REFORM

The last two years have been a time of renewed interest in the question of how government is organized. The Congress has instituted a number of reforms in its own procedures and is considering others. Judicial reform—at all levels of government—has also become a matter of intense concern. The relationship between various levels of government has attracted increased attention—and so, of course, has the subject of executive reform.

This administration, with the counsel and the cooperation of the Congress, has taken a number of steps to reorganize the executive branch of the Federal Government. We have set up a new Domestic Council and a new Office of Management and Budget in the Executive Office of the President. We have created a new Environmental Protection Agency and a new United States Postal Service. We have worked to rationalize the internal structure of Federal departments and agencies.

All of these and other changes have been important, but none has been comprehensive. And now we face a fundamental choice. We can continue to tinker with the machinery and to make constructive changes here and there— each of them bringing some marginal improvement in the Government's capacities. Or we can step back, take a careful look, and then make a concerted and sustained effort to reorganize the executive branch according to a coherent, comprehensive view of what the Federal Government of this Nation *ought* to look like in the last third of the twentieth century.

The impulse for comprehensive reorganization has been felt before in recent decades. In fact, the recommendations I am making today stem from a long series of studies which have been made under several administrations over many years. From the report of the President's Committee on Administrative Management (the Brownlow Committee) in 1937, down through the findings of the Commission on Organization of the Executive Branch of the Government (the Hoover Commission) in 1949, the President's Task Force on Government Organization in 1964, and my own Advisory Council on Executive Organization during the last two years, the principles which I am advancing today have been endorsed by a great number of distinguished students of government and management from many backgrounds and from both political parties.

I hope the Congress will now join me in concluding, with these authorities, that we should travel the course of comprehensive reform. For only if we travel that course, and travel it successfully, will we be able to answer affirmatively in our time the fundamental question posed by Alexander Hamilton as the Constitution was being debated in 1788: "whether societies of men are really capable or not of establishing good government from reflection and choice. . . ."

THE FRAGMENTATION OF FEDERAL RESPONSIBILITY

As we reflect on organizational problems in the Federal Government today, one seems to stand out above all others: the fact that the capacity to *do* things—the power to achieve goals and to solve problems—is exceedingly fragmented and broadly scattered throughout the Federal establishment. In addressing almost any of the great challenges of our time the Federal Government finds itself speaking through a wide variety of offices and bureaus, departments and agencies. Often these units trip over one another as they move to meet a common problem. Sometimes they step on one another's toes. Frequently, they behave like a series of fragmented fiefdoms—unable to focus

Federal resources or energies in a way which produces any concentrated impact.

Consider these facts:

Nine different Federal departments and twenty independent agencies are now involved in education matters. Seven departments and eight independent agencies are involved in health. In many major cities, there are at least twenty or thirty separate manpower programs, funded by a variety of Federal offices. Three departments help develop our water resources and four agencies in two departments are involved in the management of public lands. Federal recreation areas are administered by six different agencies in three departments of the government. Seven agencies provide assistance for water and sewer systems. Six departments of the government collect similar economic information—often from the same sources—and at least seven departments are concerned with international trade. While we cannot eliminate all of this diffusion, we can do a great deal to bring similar functions under common commands.

It is important that we move boldly to consolidate the major activities of the Government. The programmatic jumble has already reached the point where it is virtually impossible to obtain an accurate count of just how many Federal grant programs exist. Some estimates go as high as 1,500. Despite impressive attempts by individual legislators and by the Office of Economic Opportunity, there is still no agreement on a comprehensive list. Again and again I hear of local officials who are unable to determine how many Federal programs serve their areas or how much Federal money is coming into their communities. One reason is that the assistance comes from such a wide variety of Federal sources.

THE CONSEQUENCES OF SCATTERED RESPONSIBILITY

What are the consequences of this scattering of Federal responsibility? There are many.

In the first place, the diffusion of responsibility makes it extremely difficult to launch a coordinated attack on complex problems. It is as if the various units of an attacking army were operating under a variety of highly independent commands. When one part of the answer to a problem lies in one department and other parts lie in other departments, it is often impossible to bring the various parts together in a unified campaign to achieve a common goal.

Even our basic analysis of public needs often suffers from a piecemeal approach. Problems are defined so that they will fit within established jurisdictions and bureaucratic conventions. And the results of government action are typically measured by the degree of activity within each program rather than by the overall impact of related activities on the outside world.

The role of a given department in the policy making process can be fundamentally compromised by the way its mission is defined. The narrower the mission, the more likely it is that the department will see itself as an advocate within the administration for a special point of view. When any department or agency begins to represent a parochial interest, then its advice and support inevitably become less useful to the man who must serve *all* of the people as their President.

Even when departments make a concerted effort to broaden their perspectives, they often find it impossible to develop a comprehensive strategy for meeting public needs. Not even the best planners can set intelligent spending priorities, for example, unless they have an opportunity to consider the full array of alternative expenditures. But if one part of the problem is studied in one department and another part of the problem is studied elsewhere, who decides which element is more important? If one office considers one set of solutions and a separate agency investigates another set of solutions, who can compare the results? Too often, no official below the very highest levels of the Government has access to enough information to make such comparisons wisely. The result is that the Government often fails to make a rational distribution of its resources among a number of program alternatives.

Divided responsibility can also mean that some problems slip between the cracks and disappear from the Government's view. Everybody's business becomes nobody's business and embarrassing gaps appear which no agency attempts to fill. At other times, various Federal authorities act as rivals, competing with one another for the same piece of "turf."

Sometimes one agency will actually duplicate the work of another; for instance, the same locality may receive two or more grants for the same project. On other occasions, Federal offices will actually find themselves working at cross purposes with one another; one agency will try to preserve a swamp, for example, while another is seeking to drain it. In an effort to minimize such problems, government officials must spend enormous amounts of time and energy negotiating with one another that should be directed toward meeting people's needs. And even when they are able to work out their differences, officials often reach compromise solutions which merely represent the lowest common denominator of their original positions. Bold and original ideas are thus sacrificed in the quest for intragovernmental harmony.

Scattered responsibility also contributes to the over-centralization of public decision making. Because competing offices are often in different chains of command, it is frequently impossible for them to resolve their differences except by referring them to higher authorities, a process which can mean interminable delays. In an attempt to provide a means for resolving such differences and for providing needed coordination, an entire new layer of bureaucracy has emerged at the *interagency* level. Last year, the Office of Management and

Budget counted some 850 interagency committees. Even so, there are still many occasions when only the White House itself can resolve such interjurisdictional disputes. Too many questions thus surface at the Presidential level that should be resolved at levels of Government closer to the scene of the action.

Inefficient organization at the Federal level also undermines the effectiveness of State and local governments. Mayors and Governors waste countless hours and dollars touching base with a variety of Federal offices—each with its own separate procedures and its own separate policies. Some local officials are so perplexed by the vast array of Federal programs in a given problem area that they miss out on the very ones that would be most helpful to them. Many State and local governments find they must hire expensive specialists to guide them through the jungles of the Federal bureaucracy.

If it is confusing for lower levels of government to deal with this maze of Federal offices, that challenge can be even more bewildering for individual citizens. Whether it is a doctor seeking aid for a new health center, a businessman trying to get advice about selling in foreign markets, or a welfare recipient going from one office to another in order to take full advantage of Federal services, the people whom the Government is supposed to be serving are often forced to weave their way through a perplexing obstacle course as a condition of receiving help.

THE HOBBLING OF ELECTED LEADERSHIP

Perhaps the most significant consequence of scattered responsibility in the executive branch is the hobbling effect it has on elected leadership—and, therefore, on the basic principles of democratic government. In our political system, when the people identify a problem they elect to public office men and women who promise to solve that problem. If these leaders succeed, they can be reelected; if they fail, they can be replaced. Elections are the People's tool for keeping government responsive to their needs.

This entire system rests on the assumption, however, that elected leaders can make the government respond to the people's mandate. Too often, this assumption is wrong. When lines of responsibility are as tangled and as ambiguous as they are in many policy areas, it is extremely difficult for either the Congress or the President to see that their intentions are carried out.

If the President or the Congress wants to launch a program or change a program or even find out how a program is working, it often becomes necessary to consult with a half dozen or more authorities, each of whom can blame the others when something goes wrong. It is often impossible to delegate to any one official the full responsibility for carrying out a specific mandate, since the machinery for doing that job is divided among various agencies. As a result, there is frequently no single official—even at the Cabinet level—whom the President or the Congress can hold accountable for Government's success or failure in meeting a given need.

No wonder bureaucracy has sometimes been described as "the rule of no one." No wonder the public complains about programs which simply seem to drift. When elected officials cannot hold appointees accountable for the performance of government, then the voters' influence on government's behavior is also weakened.

HOW DID THINGS GET THIS WAY?

The American people clearly pay a very high price for the incapacities of governmental structures—one that is measured in disappointment, frustration and wasted tax dollars. But how did things get this way?

What happened, essentially, was that the organization of Government—like the grant-in-aid programs which I have discussed in my special messages to the Congress concerning revenue sharing—grew up in a haphazard, piecemeal fashion over the years. Whenever Government took on an important new assignment or identified an important new constituency, the chances were pretty good that a new organizational entity would be established to deal with it. Unfortunately, as each new office was set up, little or no attention was given to the question of how it would fit in with the old ones. Thus office was piled upon office in response to developing needs; when new needs arose and still newer units were created, the older structures simply remained in place.

Of the twelve executive departments now in existence, only five can trace their origins to the beginnings of our country. The Departments of State and Treasury were set up in 1789; so was the War Department—the predecessor of the Department of Defense. The positions of Attorney General and Postmaster General were also established in 1789, though it was not until later that the departments they head were set up in their present form. One of these five units, the Post Office Department, will soon become an independent corporation. But, under my proposals, the other four "original" departments would remain intact. It is the seven newer departments of the Government which would be affected by the changes I recommend.

These seven departments were set up to meet the changing needs of a growing nation, needs which have continued to change over the years. The Department of the Interior, for example, was established in 1849 to deal with newly opened western lands and especially with the Indians who inhabited them. The Department of Agriculture was also added in the nineteenth century, at a time when the overwhelming majority of our people were directly affected by the tremendous expansion of agricultural enterprise. In the early years of the twentieth century, in a time of rapid and unsettling industrial growth, the Department of Commerce and Labor was set up. The Labor Department was split off from it in 1913, in response to feelings that labor was suffering from an imbalance of power and needed additional influence. The three newest departments of the Government—Health, Education, and Welfare, Housing and Urban Development, and Transportation—were all created after World War II. Each represented a first step toward bringing together some of the new Federal offices and agencies which had proliferated so rapidly in recent decades.

ORGANIZING AROUND GOALS

As we look at the present organization of the Federal Government, we find that many of the existing units deal with methods and subjects rather than with purposes and goals. If we have a question about labor we go to the Labor Department and if we have a business problem we go to the Commerce Department. If we are interested in housing we go to one department and if we are interested in highways we go to another.

The problem is that as our society has become more complex, we often find ourselves using a *variety* of *means* to achieve a *single* set of *goals*. We are interested, for example, in economic development—which requires new markets, more productive workers and better transportation systems. But which department do we go to for that? And what if we want to build a new city, with sufficient public facilities, adequate housing, and decent recreation areas—which department do we petition then?

We sometimes seem to have forgotten that government is not in business to deal with subjects on a chart but to achieve real objectives for real human beings. These objectives will never be fully achieved unless we change our old ways of thinking. It is not enough merely to reshuffle departments for the sake of reshuffling them. We must rebuild the executive branch according to a new understanding of how government can best be organized to perform effectively.

The key to that new understanding is the concept that the executive branch of the government should be organized around basic goals. Instead of grouping activities by narrow subjects or by limited constituencies, we should organize them around the great purposes of government in modern society. For only when a department is set up to achieve a given set of purposes, can we effectively hold that department accountable for achieving them. Only when the responsibility for realizing basic objectives is clearly focused in a specific governmental unit, can we reasonably hope that those objectives will be realized.

When government is organized by goals, then we can fairly expect that it will pay more attention to results and less attention to procedures. Then the success of government will at last be clearly linked to the things that happen in society rather than the things that happen in government.

Under the proposals which I am submitting, those in the Federal Government who deal with common or closely related problems would work together in the same organizational framework. Each department would be given a mission broad enough so that it could set comprehensive policy directions and resolve internally the policy conflicts which are most likely to arise. The responsibilities of each department would be defined in a way that minimizes parochialism and enables the President and the Congress to hold specific officials responsible for the achievement of specific goals.

These same organizational principles would also be applied to the *internal* organization of each department. Similar functions would be grouped together within each new entity, making it still easier to delegate authority to lower levels and further enhancing the accountability of subordinate officials. In addition, the proposals I submit today include a number of improvements in the management of Federal programs, so that we can take full advantage of the opportunities afforded us by organizational restructuring.

The administration is today transmitting to the Congress four bills which, if enacted, would replace seven of the present executive departments and several other agencies with four new departments: the Department of Natural Resources, the Department of Community Development, the Department of Human Resources and the Department of Economic Affairs. A special report and summary—which explain my recommendations in greater detail—have also been prepared for each of the proposed new departments.

THE DEPARTMENT OF NATURAL RESOURCES

One of the most notable developments in public consciousness in recent years has been a growing concern for protecting the environment and a growing awareness of its highly interdependent nature. The science of ecology—the study of the interrelationships between living organisms and their environments—has experienced a sudden rise in popularity. All of us have become far more sensitive to the way in which each element of our natural habitat affects all other elements.

Unfortunately, this understanding is not yet reflected in the way our Government is organized. Various part of the *interdependent* environment are still under the purview of highly *independent* Federal offices. As a result, Federal land policies, water programs, mineral policies, forestry practices, recreation activities and energy programs cannot be easily coordinated, even though the manner in which each is carried out has a great influence on all the others.

Again and again we encounter intragovernmental conflicts in the environmental area. One department's watershed project, for instance, threatens to slow the flow of water to another department's reclamation project downstream. One agency wants to develop an electric power project on a certain river while other agencies are working to keep the same area wild. Different departments follow different policies for timber production and conservation, for grazing, for fire prevention and for recreational activities on the Federal lands they control, though the lands are often contiguous.

We cannot afford to continue in this manner. The challenges in the natural resource field have become too pressing. Some forecasts say that we will double our usage of energy in the next 10 years, of water in the next 18 years, and of metals in the next 22 years. In fact, it is predicted that the United States will use more energy and more critical resources in the remaining years of this century than in all of our history up until now. Government must perform at its very best if it is to help the Nation meet these challenges.

I propose that a new Department of Natural Resources be created that would bring together the many natural resource responsibilities now scattered throughout the Federal Government. This Department would work to conserve, manage and utilize our resources in a way that would protect the quality of the environment and achieve a true harmony between man and nature. The major activities of the new Department would be organized under its five subdivisions: Land and Recreation Resources, Water Resources, Energy and Minerals Resources, Oceanic, Atmospheric and Earth Sciences, and Indian and Territorial Affairs.

The new Department of Natural Resources would absorb the present Department of the Interior. Other major programs which would be joined to it would include: The Forest Service and the soil and water conservation programs from the Department of Agriculture, planning and funding for the civil functions of the Army Corps of Engineers and for the civilian power functions of the Atomic Energy Commission, the interagency Water Resources Council, the oil and gas pipeline safety functions of the Department of Transportation, and the National Oceanic and Atmospheric Administration from the Department of Commerce. Because of their historical association with the Department of the Interior, the programs of the Bureau of Indian Affairs would be administered by the new Department until such time as an acceptable alternative arrangement could be worked out with Indian leaders and other concerned parties.

THE DEPARTMENT OF COMMUNITY DEVELOPMENT

A restless and highly mobile people, Americans are constantly creating new communities and renewing old ones throughout our land. In an era of rapid change, this process—which once took generations—can now be repeated in just a few years.

At the same time, the process of community development is becoming even more complex, particularly as the problems of urban and rural communities begin to merge. The elements of community life are many and the mark of a cohesive community is the harmonious way in which they interrelate. That is why we hear so much these days about the importance of community planning. And that is why it is essential that Federal aid for community development be designed to meet a wide range of related needs in a highly coordinated manner.

Often this does not happen under the present system. The reason is that the basic community development programs of the Federal Government are presently divided among at least eight separate authorities—including four executive departments and four independent agencies.

A community that seeks development assistance thus finds that it has to search out aid from a variety of Federal agencies. Each agency has its own forms and regulations and timetables—and its own brand of red tape. Each has its own field organizations, often with independent and overlapping boundaries for regions and districts. Sometimes a local community must consult with Federal offices in three or four different States.

The result is that local leaders often find it virtually impossible to relate Federal assistance programs to their own local development strategies. The mayor of one small town has observed that by the time he finishes dealing with eight Federal planning agencies, he has little time to do anything else.

Occasionally, it must be admitted, a community can reap unexpected benefits from this diffusion of Federal responsibility. The story is told of one small city that applied to six different agencies for help in building a sewage treatment plant and received affirmative responses from all six. If all the grants had been completed, the community would have cleared a handsome profit—but at the Federal taxpayer's expense.

To help correct such problems, I propose that the major community development functions of the Federal Government be pulled together into a new Department of Community Development. It would be the overriding purpose of this Department to help build a wholesome and safe community environment for every American. This process would require a comprehensive series of programs which are equal to the demands of growing population and which provide for balanced growth in urban and rural areas. The new Department would operate through three major administrations: a Housing Administration, a Community Transportation Administration and an Urban and Rural Development Administration. A fourth unit, the Federal Insurance Administration, would be set up administratively by the Secretary.

The new Department of Community Development would absorb the present Department of Housing and Urban Development. Other components would include certain elements of the Economic Development Administration and the Regional Commission programs from the Department of Commerce, the independent Appalachian Regional Commission, various Department of Agriculture programs including water and waste disposal grants and loans, the

Rural Electrification Administration, and rural housing programs. The Community Action and Special Impact Programs of the Office of Economic Opportunity would be included, as would the Public Library construction grant program from the Department of Health, Education, and Welfare and certain disaster assistance functions now handled by the Office of Emergency Preparedness and the Small Business Administration. Most Federal highway programs and the Urban Mass Transportation Administration would be transferred from the present Department of Transportation.

I would note that while the Department of Transportation is a relatively new entity, it, too, is now organized around methods and not around purposes. A large part of the Department of Transportation would be moved into the new Department of Economic Affairs—but those functions which particularly support community development would be placed in the Department which is designed to meet that goal.

THE DEPARTMENT OF HUMAN RESOURCES

The price of obsolete organization is evidenced with special force in those Government programs which are directly designed to serve individuals and families. In part this is because there has been so much new legislation in the human resource field in recent decades; the old machinery is simply overstrained by its new challenges. But whatever the reasons, human resource programs comprise one area in which the Government is singularly ill-equipped to deliver adequate results.

I have already commented on the broad dispersion of Federal health and education activities. Similar examples abound. Income support programs, including those which administer food stamps, welfare payments, retirement benefits and other forms of assistance, are scattered among three departments and a number of other agencies. The Department of Agriculture, the Department of Health, Education, and Welfare, and the Office of Economic Opportunity all handle food and nutrition matters. Child care programs, migrant programs, manpower programs, and consumer programs often suffer from similarly divided attention.

In one city, two vocational training centers were built three blocks apart at about the same time and for the same purpose, with money from two different Federal agencies. And for every case of overattention, there are many more of neglect. Consider the plight of a poor person who must go to one office for welfare assistance, to another for food stamps, to another for financial counseling, to still another for legal aid, to a fifth office for employment assistance, to a sixth place for job training, and to a number of additional offices for various kinds of medical help. The social worker who might guide him through this maze often works in still another location.

Such situations are clearly intolerable, yet the Federal Government—

which ought to be working to reform these confused systems—actually is responsible for much of the confusion in the first place.

I believe that we can take a major step toward remedying such problems by establishing a new Department of Human Resources which would unify major Federal efforts to assist the development of individual potential and family well-being. This Department would be subdivided, in turn, into three major administrations: Health, Human Development, and Income Security.

This new Department would incorporate most of the present Department of Health, Education and Welfare with the following significant additions: a number of food protection, food distribution and nutrition programs from the Department of Agriculture, the College Housing program from the Department of Housing and Urban Development, the independent Railroad Retirement Board, various programs from the Office of Economic Opportunity (including nutrition, health, family planning, alcoholism, and drug rehabilitation efforts), and the Manpower Administration, the Women's Bureau, the Unemployment Insurance Program and a number of other employment service and training activities from the Department of Labor.

THE DEPARTMENT OF ECONOMIC AFFAIRS

One of the first things most students learn about economics is that the material progress of our civilization has resulted in large measure from a growing division of labor. While a single family or a single community once provided most of its own goods and services, it now specializes in providing only a few, depending increasingly on a far-flung, intricate network of other people and other organizations for its full economic well-being.

The only way the Federal Government can deal effectively with such a highly interdependent economy is by treating a wide range of economic considerations in a comprehensive and coordinated manner. And—as our Gross National Product moves beyond the trillion dollar level and as our productive system, which now accounts for approximately 40 percent of the world's wealth, encounters new challenges from other nations—it is becoming even more important that Federal economic policies be carried out as effectively as possible.

But again, the organization of the Government works against the systematic consideration of economic complexities. The step by step evolution of our Federal machinery has created a series of separate entities—each handling a separate part of the economic puzzle. Some of these entities are relatively autonomous units within departments. Others are independent agencies. But perhaps the most dramatic evidence of our fragmented approach to the economy is the existence of four major executive departments which handle highly interdependent economic matters: Commerce, Labor, Agriculture, and Transportation.

This situation can seriously impair governmental efforts to respond effectively to economic challenges. One department, for example, may be concerned with the raw materials a given industry receives from the farms, while a second department is concerned with getting these materials to the factory and getting the product to its market. Meanwhile, a third department is concerned with the workers who harvest the crops, run the transportation systems and manufacture the product, while a fourth department is concerned with the businessmen who own the plant where the product is made and the stores where it is merchandised.

Such a division of responsibility can also create a great deal of overlap. The Agriculture Department, for instance, finds that its interest in agricultural labor is shared by the Labor Department, its regard for agricultural enterprise is shared by the Small Business Administration, and its concern for providing sufficient transportation for farm products is shared by the Department of Transportation. The Commerce, Labor and Agriculture Departments duplicate one another in collecting economic statistics, yet they use computers and statistical techniques which are often incompatible.

It has sometimes been argued that certain interest groups need a department to act as their special representative within the Government. In my view, such an arrangement serves the best interests of neither the special group nor the general public. Little is gained and much can be lost, for example, by treating our farmers or our workers or other groups as if they are independent participants in our economic life. Their problems cannot be adequately treated in isolation; their well-being is intimately related to the way our entire economy functions.

I would not suggest these reforms if I thought they would in any way result in the neglect of farmers, workers, minorities or any other significant groups within our country. To the contrary, I propose these reforms because I am convinced they will enable us to serve these groups much better. Under my proposals, the new Department of Economic Affairs would be in a much stronger position really to *do* something about the wide-ranging factors which influence farm income than is the present Department of Agriculture, for example. It could do more to meet the complex needs of workingmen and women than can the present Department of Labor. It would be able to pull together a wider range of resources to help minority businessmen than can the present Department of Commerce.

Federal organization in the economic area has been the target of frequent criticism over the years. During the previous administration alone, two special studies of executive organization recommended that it be substantially altered. I have received a similar recommendation from my Advisory Council on Executive Organization.

I am therefore recommending to the Congress that a new Department of Economic Affairs be established to promote economic growth, to foster economic justice, and to encourage more efficient and more productive relationships among the various elements of our economy and between the United States economy and those of other nations. As this single new Department joined the Treasury Department, the Council of Economic Advisers and the Federal Reserve Board in shaping economic policy, it would speak with a stronger voice and would offer a more effective, more highly integrated viewpoint than four different departments can possibly do at present. The activities of the new Department would be grouped under the following six administrations: Business Development, Farms and Agriculture, Labor Relations and Standards, National Transportation, Social, Economic, and Technical Information and International Economics.

The new Department of Economic Affairs would include many of the offices that are now within the Departments of Commerce, Labor and Agriculture. A large part of the Department of Transportation would also be relocated here, including the United States Coast Guard, the Federal Railroad Administration, the St. Lawrence Seaway Development Corporation, the National Transportation Safety Board, the Transportation Systems Center, the Federal Aviation Administration, the Motor Carrier Safety Bureau and most of the National Highway Traffic Safety Administration. The Small Business Administration, the Science Information Exchange program from the Smithsonian Institution, the National Institute for Occupational Health and Safety from the Department of Health, Education, and Welfare and the Office of Technology Utilization from the National Aeronautics and Space Administration would also be included in the new Department.

OTHER ORGANIZATIONAL REFORMS

Regrouping functions *among* departments can do a great deal to enhance the effectiveness of government. It should be emphasized, however, that regrouping functions *within* departments is also a critical part of my program for executive reform. Just as like tasks are grouped together within a given department, so similar operations should be rationally assembled within subordinate units. Such a realignment of functions, in and of itself, would make it much easier for appointed officials to manage their agencies and for both the President and the Congress to see that their intentions are carried out.

Toward this same end, I am recommending to the Congress a number of additional steps for bringing greater managerial discipline into Government. In the first place, I am proposing that the Department Secretary and his office be considerably strengthened so that the man whom the President appoints to run a department has both the authority and the tools to run it effectively. The Secretary would be given important managerial discretion that he does not always enjoy today, including the ability to appoint many key department officials, to delegate authority to them and to withdraw or change such delegations of authority, and to marshal and deploy the resources at his command so that he can readily focus the talent available to him at the point of greatest need.

Each of the new Secretaries would be provided with a Deputy Secretary and two Under Secretaries to help him meet his responsibilities. In addition, each major program area within a department would be headed by a high-level administrator who would be responsible for effectively managing a particular group of related activities. These officials would be appointed by the President and their appointments would be subject to Senate confirmation.

It is my philosophy that we should give clear assignments to able leaders— and then be sure that they are equipped to carry them out. As a part of this same effort, we should do all we can to give the best new management tools to those who run the new departments. There is no better time to introduce needed procedural changes *within* departments than a time of structural change *among* departments. We can reap great benefits if we take advantage of this opportunity by implementing the most advanced techniques and equipment for such tasks as planning and evaluation, data collection, systematic budgeting, and personnel administration.

Finally, I would again stress in this message—as I have in my discussions of revenue sharing—the importance of decentralizing government activities as much as possible. As I have already observed, the consolidation of domestic departments would do a great deal to facilitate decentralization, since it would produce fewer interagency disputes that require resolution at higher levels. It is also true, as many management experts have pointed out, that as the reliability and scope of information expand at higher levels of government, officials can delegate authority to lower levels with greater confidence that it will be used well.

In addition to the consolidation of functions, I am also proposing a reform of the field structures of the Federal Government that would also promote decentralization. Each Department, for example, would appoint a series of Regional Directors who would represent the Secretary with respect to all Department activities in the field. Planning, coordination and the resolution of conflicts could thus be more readily achieved without Washington's involvement, since there would be a "Secretarial presence" at the regional level. Further coordination at lower levels of government would be provided by strengthening the ten Regional Councils which include as members the Regional Directors of various departments in a given area of the country.

In the first months of my administration I moved to establish common regional boundaries and regional headquarters for certain domestic departments. I observed at that time that the Federal Government has never given adequate attention to the way in which its departments are organized to carry out their missions in the field. It is now time that we remedied this pattern of neglect. Even the best organized and best managed departments in Washington cannot serve the people adequately if they have to work through inadequate field structures.

Industry and government both have found that even the largest organizations can be run effectively when they are organized according to rational principles and managed according to sound techniques. There is nothing mystical about these principles or these techniques; they can be used to make the Federal Government far more effective in a great many areas.

As we consolidate and rationalize Federal functions, as we streamline and modernize our institutional architecture, as we introduce new managerial techniques and decentralize Government activities, we will give Government the capacity to operate far more efficiently than it does today. It will be able to do more work with fewer mechanisms and fewer dollars. It will be able to use its work force more productively. This could mean significant savings for our taxpayers. I would emphasize, however, that any reductions in the Federal work force attributable to this proposal would come by normal turnover; no civil servant should lose his job as a result of this plan.

It is important that these reforms be seen by our civil servants not as a threat to their security but as an opportunity for greater achievement. We have worked hard to bring able people into Government employment. Executive reorganization can help the Nation make even better use of their talent and their dedication and it can also make it easier for us to attract more men and women of great vision and competence into public service at the Federal level.

FOCUSING POWER WHERE IT CAN BE USED BEST

These proposals for reorganizing the Federal Government are a natural complement to my proposals for revenue sharing; there is a sense in which these two initiatives represent two sides of the same coin. Both programs can help us decentralize government, so that more decisions can be made at levels closer to the people. More than that, both programs are concerned with restoring the general capacity of government to meet its responsibilities.

On the one hand, through revenue sharing, we would give back to the States and localities those functions which belong at the State and local level. To help them perform those functions more effectively, we would give them more money to spend and more freedom in spending it. At the same time, however, we must also do all we can to help the Federal Government handle as effectively as possible those functions which belong at the Federal level. Executive reorganization can help us achieve this end by bringing together related activities which are now fragmented and scattered.

A healthy Federal system is one in which we neither disperse power for the sake of dispersing it nor concentrate power for the sake of concentrating it. Instead, a sound Federal system requires us to *focus* power at that place where it can be used to the greatest public advantage. This means that each level of government must be assigned those tasks which it can do best and must be given the means for carrying out those assignments.

THE CENTRAL QUESTION

Ever since the first settlers stepped upon our shores more than three centuries ago, a central question of the American experience has been: How do we best organize our government to meet the needs of the people? That was the central question as the colonists set up new governments in a new world. It was the central question when they broke from their mother country and made a new nation. It was the central question as they wrote a new Constitution in 1787 and, at each critical turning point since that time, it has remained a dominant issue in our national experience.

In the last forty years, as the Federal Government has grown in scope and complexity, the question of how it should be organized has been asked with even greater intensity and relevance. During this time, we have moved to formulate responsive answers to this question in an increasingly systematic manner. Searching studies of Government management and organization have been made under virtually every national administration since the 1930s and many needed reforms have resulted.

What is now required, however, is a truly comprehensive restructuring of executive organization, one that is commensurate with the growth of the Nation and the expansion of the government. In the last twenty years alone our population has increased by one-third and the Federal budget has quintupled. In the last two decades, the number of Federal civilian employees has risen by almost 30 percent and the domestic programs they administer have multiplied tenfold. Three executive departments and fourteen independent agencies have been tacked on to the Federal organization chart during that brief span.

Yet it still is the same basic organization chart that has set the framework of governmental action for decades. While there have been piecemeal changes, there has been no fundamental overhaul. Any business that grew and changed so much and yet was so patient with old organizational forms would soon go bankrupt. The same truth holds in the public realm. Public officials cannot be patient with outmoded forms when the people have grown so impatient with government.

Thomas Jefferson once put it this way: "I am certainly not an advocate for frequent and untried changes in laws and constitutions," he wrote, "but . . . laws and institutions must go hand in hand with the progress of the human mind. As that becomes more developed, more enlightened, as new discoveries are made, new truths disclosed, and manners and opinions change with the change of circumstances, institutions must advance also, and keep pace with the times."

"*Institutions must advance.*" Jefferson and his associates saw that point clearly in the late 18th century, and the fruit of their vision was a new nation. It is now for us—if our vision matches theirs—to renew the Government they created and thus give new life to our common dreams.

Document 4

Plans for the Second Term

The President's Remarks to Reporters at Camp David on His Plans for Changes in the Cabinet, Sub-Cabinet, and White House Staff. November 27, 1972

Ladies and gentlemen, as you have been here at Camp David for the past 2 weeks, I know that you would like somewhat an evaluation of what has happened up to this time and some projection as to the future, so that you can know how to cover our activities between now and the time the Congress reconvenes.

I have had the opportunity over the past 2 weeks to meet now with all the members of the Cabinet and with all of the senior members of the White House Staff. All of those meetings, as you know, have taken place at Camp David.

The decisions with regard to the members of the next Cabinet will be announced beginning tomorrow. They will be announced over a period of time, and I think that all of the announcements will be concluded before the 15th of December. As far as the order in which they are announced, you should draw no connotations from that, because that depends in some instances upon whether we have completed the Congressional consultation which is necessary when Cabinet appointments are being made, and also, in other cases, whether we have completed the evaluation of appointments to the sub-Cabinet. Those appointments, as you will note as time goes on here during the next 2 or 3 weeks, become increasingly important in our plans for the operations of the Cabinet, and particularly its relationship with the White House Staff.

I think a word would be in order as to why we do have you at Camp David, why these meetings could not have taken place in the comfort of the White House press room, and for that matter, the Oval Office.

I thought it would be interesting to recap for you in a moment the times that I have been here, and why we will be using Camp David for activities of this type and other major decisions that will be made by the Administration over the next 4 years.

Looking over the past 4 years, I have written most of my major speeches here, the speech of November 3, the speech of May 8 with regard to the bombing and mining of Haiphong. A number of the major decisions have been made at Camp David, the August 15 economic decision in 1971. For example, the major budget meeting of this year, the budget for the next fiscal year, will be held this Thursday at Camp David.

The reason for that is not that the facilities here are any better than those at the White House—as a matter of fact I suppose the White House facilities in some respects, even for members of the Cabinet who come here, might be better—but the reason is that I find, and each individual, of course, who holds the position which I hold must work in the way that it best fits his own patterns, I find that getting away from the White House, from the Oval Office, from that 100 yards that one walks every day from the President's bedroom to the President's Office or the extra 50 yards across to the EOB, getting away gives a sense of perspective which is very, very useful.

I developed that pattern early in the Administration and am going to follow it even more during the next 4 years. We know that in all walks of life, even in the case of you ladies and gentlemen of the press, that one constantly has the problem of either getting on top of the job or having the job get on top of you.

I find that up here on top of a mountain it is easier for me to get on top of the job, to think in a more certainly relaxed way at times—although the work has been very intensive in these past 2 weeks as it was before the other great decisions that have been made here—but also in a way in which one is not interrupted either physically or personally or in any other way, and can think objectively with perception about the problems that he has to make decisions on.

As far as the Cabinet members are concerned, I asked them to do exactly the same thing over these past 2 weeks or two and a half weeks since the election. I asked each of them to leave his office or his home for a period of time to think about his department, to think also about his own role in Government, and then have a discussion with me with regard to how we could do a better job over the next 4 years than we have done over the past 4 years.

It has been interesting to note that each member of the Cabinet, virtually to a man, has said that having that opportunity, as a matter of fact, being directed to take that opportunity, proved to be valuable. Each has come back with recommendations for reorganization of his own department, each has come back with recommendations for very significant cuts in expenditures, and significant cuts in personnel, which had not been considered possible in the prior budget rundown which took place about a month ago. And each, of course, had had an opportunity to think of his own role, what he would want it to be in the period ahead.

Now, with regard to the members of the Cabinet and what decisions you may expect as to those announcements let me, without divulging what any of the decisions are now, because they will be made over the next couple of weeks, let me tell you what generally has been the pattern.

Some members of the Cabinet—Secretary Laird, Secretary Romney, of course, come to mind—had indicated before the election that they desired to leave Government after their first 4 years. Those desires, of course, we have accepted, but with regret, because I would like to say that I consider every member of the Cabinet a valuable member of our team. I consider each one of them one who is a very valuable public servant, and every one of them, even those who have left, has been given the opportunity to remain in Government service in some very high capacity.

But as I have indicated, some had made the decision, and that decision has been respected, to leave Government service. Others felt that they could better serve by changing their position, by moving from one Cabinet position to another Cabinet position, or from a Cabinet position to another position in another area of Government with similar responsibility.

Without divulging what the eventual decision with regard to his future is, a good example of this is Caspar Weinberger, the Director of OMB. I remember, when he first took the job as Budget Director, he said that no one should be a Budget Director for more than 2 years, because by that time he wears himself out and he is unable to look at the job objectively from that time on. Mr. Weinberger will leave that position. I have prevailed upon him to accept another position. That will be one of the announcements that will be made in the course of the next few days.

But that same pattern repeated itself in a variety of ways with other members of the Cabinet and of the White House Staff as I talked to them.

A word, too, with regard to the White House Staff. Several changes will be made. I felt from the beginning that it was important that the White House establish the example for the balance of the Government in terms of cutting down on personnel, doing a better job with fewer people. Consequently, while there will be cuts in personnel across the Government, throughout the departments, the biggest cuts will be made in the White House Staff itself.

We have been able to do that for a number of reasons, but the most fundamental one is that we are going to put greater responsibility on individual Cabinet members for various functions that previously have been that of the White House Staff.

The White House Staff has rather grown like Topsy. It has grown in every administration. It is now time to reverse that growth to do a more effective job, by bringing the Cabinet members into closer contact with the White House, of course, with the President himself. This will become more apparent as the various appointments are announced, and as our plans on reorganization are announced.

The other point that I should make is that there has been some speculation to the effect that there is a move here on the top of this mountain to, as a result of the rather significant victory of November 7, to reach out and grasp a lot of power and draw it into the White House and to the executive department. Exactly the opposite is the case.

What we are trying to do is to find a way to make our Government more responsive to people, and the way to make it more responsive to people across this country is not to concentrate more and more power in one office, but to have that power given to and delegated to, where it possibly can, to responsible members of the Administration team in the Cabinet, in the White House, or in other agencies of the Government.

I think a final point that I might make has to do with the reasons for changing at all. I have covered this in an interview I gave immediately after the election, but I might elaborate on it for just a moment with you ladies and gentlemen here at Camp David.

My study of elections in this country, and of second terms particularly, is that second terms almost inevitably are downhill; not always—for example, in Woodrow Wilson's case, he had a very significant first term on the domestic scene, and then the war, World War I, came along in the second term. No one would have known what would have happened in the second term had that crisis not come along.

But generally speaking, whether they are Democratic administrations or Republican administrations, the tendency is for an administration to run out of steam after the first 4 years, and then to coast, and usually coast downhill. That is particularly true when there is what you call a landslide victory. As I have put it to some of my closest colleagues, generally when you think of a landslide, you are submerged by it and you also think in terms of a landslide pushing you downhill.

What I am trying to do is to change that historical pattern. The only way that historical pattern can be changed is to change not only some of the players, but also some of the plays, if I may use the analogy to sports. What I am suggesting here is that when a new administration comes in, it comes in with new ideas, new people, new programs. That is why it has vitality and excitement. That is why oftentimes it has change which is very helpful to the country, and progress.

A second administration usually lacks that vitality. It lacks it not because the men and the women in the administration are any less dedicated, but because it is inevitable when an individual has been in a Cabinet position or, for that matter, holds any position in Government, after a certain length of time he becomes an advocate of the status quo; rather than running the bureaucracy, the bureaucracy runs him.

It has been my conviction for years that elected officials in this country too often become prisoners of what we would call the bureaucracy which they are supposed to run. This is no reflection on the bureaucracy. There are millions of dedicated people working for government throughout this country who are not elected officials or people who are appointed by the elected officials.

It is, however, simply a statement of fact that it is the responsibility of those who are elected to the highest office in this land to see to it that what they consider to be the directions that the people want them to follow are followed out and not that they simply come in and continue to go along doing things as they have been done in the past.

I do not consider the election of November 7, 1972, despite the rather massive majority, to have been simply an approval of things as they were. I do not consider that election to have been an endorsement of the status quo. That is completely contrary to the American tradition. This is not a stand-still country. It is a go-ahead country. That is our tradition from the beginning. The American people are never satisfied with things as they are. The American people want change. In my view, as I have often stated, I think they want change that works, not radical change, not destructive change, but change that builds rather than destroys. It is that kind of change that I have tried to stand for and I will continue to work for over these next 4 years.

But when we look at the election of 1972, we must recognize that it came after a year of very significant change: the Moscow summit, the Peking summit, and in the domestic field—while we had many disappointments—the revenue sharing, which will have such a massive effect on the relationships between Federal and State governments. But after that year of '72 in which we had had very significant change internationally and to a lesser extent on the domestic front, the American people, in voting, I think, for the present Administration, were not voting to stand still but to go ahead with that kind of imaginative change.

So, I think you can expect the next administration to be one that will have some new players. We will have some new plays, although we will consider this to be not a game, but very, very serious public business.

But we feel that we have a mandate, a mandate not simply for approval of what we have done in the past, but a mandate to continue to provide change that will work in our foreign policy and in our domestic policy, change that will build a better life, that will mean progress at home toward our great goals here, just as we have been making progress in the field of international affairs.

I will conclude simply by saying that Ron Ziegler will make the announcements here from Camp David. I will be here, of course, at the Camp, meeting with a number of sub-Cabinet people and others over the next 2 weeks, and as those announcements are made, you will have the opportunity to talk to each of the members of the Cabinet and the sub-Cabinet and to interview them.

Of course, those who have to come up for confirmation, and there will be several in that category, will not be able to answer any questions except in a very general sense.

With regard to specific names, I think it would be well to remove from the speculation two names I have noticed in the press. I did meet, as you know, with Governor Connally and with Governor Rockefeller. I believe that Governor Connally and Governor Rockefeller would be very valuable members of any Cabinet.

After discussions with them, I found that each would prefer at this time not to take a full-time Cabinet or Government position. However, I am glad to say that each has agreed to continue to serve on the Foreign Intelligence Advisory Board, and each has agreed to undertake special part-time assignments, Governor Connally in the field of international economic affairs where he has particular experience and capability, and Governor Rockefeller in the field of domestic affairs where he is undertaking some very intensive and very important research work in the development of our urban policies.

Thank you.

Document 5

Nixon Looks Ahead: "A New Feeling of Responsibility . . . of Self-discipline"

Garnett D. Horner, *The Washington Star-News*, November 9, 1972

President Nixon, promising the American people the rigors of self-reliance instead of the soft life, says he hopes to use his second term to lead the nation out of a crisis of the spirit.

In an interview with the Star-News, the President vowed to work to end "the whole era of permissiveness" and to nurture "a new feeling of responsibility, a new feeling of self-discipline."

". . . We have passed through a very great spiritual crisis in this country," he said. He added that the Vietnam war was "blamed for it totally" by many but he said the war was really "only part of the problem and in many cases was only an excuse rather than a reason."

With a puritan fervor he has seldom shown in public, Nixon seemed to be closing the door on a time in which he felt the nation had been pampered and indulged, leaving its character weakened.

"The average American," he said, "is just like the child in the family. You give him some responsibility and he is going to amount to something. He is going to do something.

"If, on the other hand, you make him completely dependent and pamper him and cater to him too much, you are going to make him soft, spoiled and eventually a very weak individual."

He had just come through a campaign, the President recalled, in which he "didn't go out with a whole bag full of goodies." And he made it clear that there will be few social goodies in his second administration.

He singled out the federal payroll as a prime target for his attention in the new term. He said that some departments are "too fat, too bloated" and that civilian Defense Department employes "are getting in the way of each other." His remedy: a thinning out all through the government, including the White House.

Nixon noted suggestions that, no longer facing the problem of reelection, he might now be more free to advocate massive new social programs aimed at curing the nation's domestic ills.

"Nothing," he said, "could be further from the mark."

He predicted, however, that the next four years would be an exciting period for Americans—on the international front because "we are going to continue to play a great role in the world" and domestically because of his determination to build a new national spirit.

Nixon said that his general approach to the presidency "is probably that of a Disraeli conservative—a strong foreign policy, strong adherence to basic values that the nation believes in and people believe in. . . ."

Repeatedly, during the conversation of nearly an hour last Sunday at his San Clemente office, Nixon indicated the conservative course—he called it basically centrist—he was charting for the next four years:

- "This country has enough on its plate in the way of huge new spending programs, social programs, throwing dollars at problems. . . . Reform, using money more effectively, will be the mark of this administration.
- "I honestly believe that government in Washington is too big and is too expensive. . . . We can do the job better with fewer people.
- "I am convinced that the total tax burden of the American people, federal, state and local, has reached the breaking point. It can go no higher.
- "It is our responsibility to find a way to reform our government institutions so that this new spirit of independence, self-reliance, pride that I sense in the American people can be nurtured."

In addition to setting the over-all tone for his next four years, the President dealt with a wide range of specific subjects. Some highlights:

Vietnam—He is "completely confident we are going to have a settlement" there. "You can bank on it."

The Election—It was settled the day Sen. McGovern was nominated by the Democrats. McGovern's views "probably did not represent even a majority of Democrats. They certainly represented a minority of the country."

Foreign policy—The second round of arms limitations talks with Russia—

SALT II—starting this month will be more important than SALT I. The Middle East "will have a very high priority." Our policy toward Cuba will not change unless Castro changes his attitude.

Domestic policy—He will "shuck off" and "trim down" social programs set up in the 1960's that he considers massive failures largely because they just "threw money at the problems."

Taxes—"There will be no solutions of problems that require a tax increase." He is convinced that the tax burden of Americans has reached "the breaking point" and can go no higher.

The courts—He intends to continue to appoint conservative judges. "The Courts . . . need men like Rehnquist and Burger and Blackmun and Powell."

His aides—Some healthy "friction, competition" between Henry Kissinger and the State Department and John Ehrlichman and the domestic agencies is going to continue. "That is the way it is going to have to be with them or their successors."

Political campaigns—They are too long and they "bore people to death." Shorter campaigns would be better for presidential candidates "because we don't want to wear our people down to a frazzle before they take on the awesome responsibilities of this position."

The President was firm in his statements but relaxed in manner as he talked. Wearing a maroon sport coat and gray slacks, he sat in a blue-upholstered easy chair and occasionally propped a foot on a table in front of him as he faced a big picture window looking out over the Pacific Ocean. To emphasize a point, he frequently hammered a hand up and down.

Nixon was perhaps most emphatic in asserting "I honestly believe that government in Washington is too big and it is too expensive."

He conceded that it is difficult to reduce the number of federal workers. But he said "you can be sure that we are going to make an effort."

He stressed that thinning "is going to cut across the board, including the White House staff. No agencies are going to be exempt in this respect."

As it has under most recent presidents, the White House staff has grown during Nixon's first term. But, he declared, "we can do a better job with fewer people. We have got to set the example on the White House staff."

He said there are some areas—in drug abuse prevention, law enforcement and social security, for example—where employe needs grow as the population grows. He also exempted "military personnel" and weapons from anything but "minimal" cuts.

"But in terms of the masses of civilian employes who are getting in the way of each other over in the Pentagon and around the country, they are going to have to take a thinning down," the President declared.

Noting that "there is a huge turn-over in government to begin with," he indicated hope that attrition through retirements and resignations will make it unnecessary to fire many government workers. "We are going to try to do it in a way that will consider the individual, but we have to accomplish the objective," he said.

He made clear that he was talking about cutting some program work as well as workers out of such agencies as HUD, HEW and the Transportation Department that he said "are all too fat, too bloated."

These relatively new departments, he went on, "came in and they did some good things, but we have to look at not only what they are doing right but at some of the things that they are doing that haven't proved out."

He said he has his Domestic Council checking what can be reformed. In programs to continue, he added, "we are going to find ways to do them with less people."

The President advanced no specific solutions to domestic problems in such areas as the cities, housing, education and health care, which some Americans believe defy conservative solutions.

But he said that if he gets "proper support" in Congress, his administration will accomplish "more significant reform" than any since Franklin D. Roosevelt's reforms—but "in a different direction."

"Roosevelt's reforms led to bigger and bigger power in Washington," he said. "It was perhaps needed then. The country's problems were so massive they couldn't be handled otherwise.

"The reforms that we are instituting are ones which will diffuse the power throughout the country and which will make [federal] government leaner, but in a sense will make it stronger. After all, fat government is weak, weak in handling the problems."

Nixon emphasized, too, that "I feel very strongly—you can't take an extreme right position that if you ignore them the problems will go away."

He added that his Domestic Council is making "the most intensive study" to pave the way for him to present to Congress next year "solutions to these problems that we think can more effectively deal with them."

There will be some modifications, too, in the recommendations he made to the last Congress, he said.

Basic to his approach to future problem solving, the President made clear, is that "there will be no solutions or problems that require a tax increase."

Even if he felt that spending more money was the best way to solve a problem, he couldn't go down that line "because more important than more money to solve a problem is to avoid a tax increase," he said.

The total tax burden cannot go higher, he said, adding that if it does "I believe we will do much to destroy the incentives which produce the progress we seek."

Nixon strongly indicated that he does not go along with the fear of some people that there is a dangerous swing to the right in the country.

Taking a poke at what he called the "limousine liberal set" of the northeast, the President said the "liberal establishment" had thought he was "out of touch with the country" for the past four years. But "that is not true," he said. He made clear he thought the election would demonstrate that it wasn't true.

He said his position was not "over on the far right" but "basically . . . simply in the center" in standing for a strong national defense, for peace with honor in Vietnam, against busing for racial balance, against permissiveness, against amnesty for draft dodgers and deserters, against legalizing marijuana.

The President spoke with deep feeling about his desire to "exert that kind of leadership" required to make all Americans proud of their country.

"I think that the tragedy of the '60's," he said, "is that so many Americans, and particularly so many young Americans, lost faith in their country, in the American system, in their country's foreign policy.

"Many were influenced to believe that they should be ashamed of our country's foreign policy, and what we were doing in the world. . . .

"Many Americans got the impression that this was an ugly country, racist, not compassionate, and part of the reason for this was the tendency of some to take every mole that we had and to make it look like a cancer."

Conceding that this country isn't perfect—"that there is much that is wrong that needs to be corrected"—he referred to his world travels and said he knew no young person abroad who wouldn't rather be here if he had the chance.

He disavowed any feeling that Americans should take pride in their country "on blind faith." He said "we want them to know why this country is right."

He said he thinks his trips this year to Peking and Moscow led people to see that "the United States was leading the world in peace" and so built pride in the American role in foreign policy.

At home, he said "I think we will re-instill some of the faith that has been lost in the '60s" as the country moves toward equality of opportunity for all, toward meeting problems of the environment, and making progress in the health and education fields.

In discussing the nation's "spiritual crisis" he put the blame largely on a "breakdown in frankly what I would call the leadership class in this country." He said, for example, that "the enormous movement toward permissiveness which led to the escalation in crime . . . came as a result of those of us who have basically a responsibility of leadership not recognizing that above everything else you must not weaken a people's character."

Here he volunteered a reiteration of his intention to continue to "appoint conservative judges to the courts . . . not reactionary judges but men who are constitutional conservatives, because the trend had gone too far in the other direction."

He stressed that "I do not mean we turn to reaction . . . to an attitude which does not have compassion toward those who cannot be blamed for some of the problems they have."

Then came a vigorous affirmation of what seems to be a central core of Nixon philosophy.

He said he felt sure some of his ideas would be "tut-tutted" by "the Georgetown cocktail set" that honestly believes the answer to problems always is some massive government program.

But he stressed a strong belief that the election would demonstrate that "the American people will thrive upon a new feeling of responsibility, a new feeling of self-discipline, rather than go back to the thoughts of the '60s that it was government's job every time there was a problem, to make people more and more dependent upon it, to give way to their whims."

"Another thing this election is about," he went on, "is whether we should move toward more massive hand-outs to people, making the people more and more dependent, or whether we say, no, it is up to you. The people are going to have to carry their share of the load."

Document 6

Tax Aid to the Poor—Reconsidered

Richard P. Nathan, *The Wall Street Journal*, April 24, 1974

The negative income tax, praised by economists and welfare theorists of all stripes when it first surfaced a few years ago as probably the most practical and humane solution to the nation's welfare problem, seems about to make a reappearance.

NIT, first proposed in 1969, is a cash-only assistance program to replace all existing welfare programs with a single system integrated with the "positive" federal income tax and typically administered nationally by the Internal Revenue Service. The consensus among Nixon watchers is that the administration is readying just such a plan for unveiling within the next six weeks.

Although I believe the administration's "New Federalism" program in domestic affairs has much to commend it, I am impressed by a growing body of evidence—both tactical and substantive—that an NIT plan to overhaul and unify all welfare programs along the lines currently being considered by Mr. Nixon's planners is not a good idea in 1974.

BAD TIMING

I'm not alone in this belief. Breaks are beginning to occur in ranks of economists who had formerly backed the negative income tax. And groups devoted to social reform also are coming increasingly to the view that they too should vote "No" on NIT. Just as this scene is shifting, perhaps not surprisingly in this ill-starred period for President Nixon, the administration appears ready to put forward such a plan. But it would be the wrong approach and at the wrong time, both for President Nixon and social policy.

Why, from President Nixon's standpoint? Since the broad hint of an NIT in his State of the Union Message, and as a reaction to many speculative news stories and leaks since then, conservatives have adamantly objected to a Nixon NIT. Yet it is just these groups that President Nixon will need most in the climax of Watergate. Politically, an NIT cannot help Richard Nixon in 1974.

Moreover, regardless of politics, an NIT is the wrong social policy in 1974 for anyone sincerely interested in helping the poor. In this connection, we need to look at some history. When the Family Assistance Plan (FAP) was advanced in 1969, there was a very serious gap in the coverage of the poor under federally aided welfare programs. The Family Assistance Plan had important characteristics that are the same as a negative income tax but was significantly less comprehensive in its proposed coverage. For example, it did not cover single persons, childless couples or the aged. The main group which it would have added to coverage was the working poor—that is, intact families where the family head is working at a low income.

These families headed by males where both the mother and father were present in the home received no benefits at all in some states in 1969 no matter how low their income was. In other states, they were aided only if the breadwinner was out of work. Thus, most poor families with two parents were left out of the welfare picture, whereas broken families were assisted in all states under AFDC (the problem-ridden Aid for Families with Dependent Children program.)

But all of this was changed by the federal food stamp program, which provides aid to all needy families, including those headed by a working male parent. A virtual pilot program assisting around 2 million persons in a few counties five years ago, the food stamp program today assists over 13 million persons and is universally available.

The dramatic growth of the food stamp program is *the single most impor-*

tant welfare change in America since the passage of the Social Security Act of 1935. Food stamps today provide more aid to working poor families than they would have received had President Nixon's Family Assistance Plan been enacted in 1972 when it died in the 92nd Congress. Furthermore, food stamp benefits are adjusted automatically every six months according to the price of food which typically goes up faster than the overall price level. Federal food stamp expenditures will soon be running at $5 billion annually and, according to one estimate, could go as high as $10 billion in 1976.

In sum, conditions are very different today than when President Nixon's FAP plan was put forward in August 1969. This is true for essentially two reasons: (1) Male-headed families now have coverage, although in many cases it is not adequate, and (2) total welfare-program growth in this period has been tremendous.

As regards the latter point, federal spending for all of what are called "income support" programs (this includes Social Security, Medicaid, Medicare, food stamps and housing subsidies) rose by 120% from 1969 to 1974, compared to a 50% rise from 1964 to 1969. The 1975 budget projects federal spending for all "income support" programs (about 55% of which is for the poor) at over $100 billion. This function alone accounts for one-half of the civilian budget of the federal government and by itself is larger than defense spending as projected for fiscal year 1975.

What's more, since Census Bureau figures do not reflect in-kind transfer (such as food stamps and Medicaid) and since welfare cash payments are generally under-counted, the contribution of these programs to the well-being of the nation's poor is not adequately reflected in available income statistics.

Taking all of these and other factors into account, there are five reasons why an NIT in 1974 is not a good idea for those concerned about meeting the needs of the poor.

First and foremost, we don't have the *FAP gap* for male-headed families that we had five years ago, although we do need to improve benefits for many working-poor families.

Second, in this politically difficult period, it makes no sense to raise the divisive issue of an NIT with its multi-billion-dollar price tag. In this regard, the lessons of the Family Assistance Plan are instructive. The Pandora's Box of emotional issues which it opened had a great deal to do with its ultimate defeat.

Third, and perhaps most important of all, there is what one expert calls *"the NIT dilemma."* The disturbing, but compelling arithmetic of every NIT plan I have seen that is politically feasible in terms of its costs is such that it would *hurt* millions among the poor by cutting their benefits. This is especially true for families headed by females and the children in those families.

Fourth, the kind of welfare crisis needed to bring together a coalition for major reform does not exist today. In my view, the theoreticians of welfare are much more concerned about conceptual neatness and program symmetry than they should be. A lack of neatness in current welfare programs is no national crisis.

Fifth, there *is* a better way. If our aim is to fill the remaining gaps and generally to promote greater equity and fairness in welfare programs for working-age persons and their families, I believe we can achieve these goals better through a series of lesser legislative changes than with an NIT.

AN INCREMENTAL STRATEGY

For example, I am intrigued by the possibility of an *"incremental strategy,"* which does such things as (1) standardize and expand unemployment insurance; (2) institute a national minimum for benefit levels for AFDC families; (3) create more jobs for unemployed family heads; (4) achieve program coordination through mandatory state (as opposed to county) administration, using common rules and definitions for all welfare programs that aid working-age persons, and (5) possibly also provide a work bonus or housing allowance for the working poor to supplement food stamps.

This is the kind of a reform agenda which needs to be fully developed and debated as an alternative to an NIT should the Nixon administration ultimately decide to advance such a plan. Times and conditions have changed. The advocates of an NIT need to take another reading of the tea leaves of social policy.

Document 7

No to Block Grants for Welfare*

Richard P. Nathan, *Common Sense*, Winter 1980

Welfare policy cannot be viewed in isolation from other fields of domestic policy. A major purpose of this article is to show that during the Nixon and Ford Administrations, a sensible framework emerged that, while not widely recognized, reflects a philosophy and strategy for domestic policymaking that can be associated with a broad band of opinion in the Republican Party.

Two ideas are key to this thesis. One, which was advanced dramatically in the Nixon-Ford period, is *decentralization*—the idea that the domestic policies

*Reprinted courtesy of the Republican National Committee's Advisory Council on Human Concerns.

of the federal government should strengthen local decisionmaking and build up the role of individual citizens. The chosen instruments for achieving this objective have been revenue sharing and block grants—broadly defined grant-in-aid programs with relatively few strings attached under which funds are distributed on an automatic formula basis. The biggest of these programs is the general revenue sharing program under which nearly $7 billion are distributed annually. Despite nibbling away at the edges by the Carter Administration by proposing narrow-gauged categorical grant-in-aid programs, this popular viewpoint stressing decentralization still remains a strong tenet of current federal grant-in-aid programs.

The second idea of domestic policy that came out of the seventies is that there must be, to the fullest extent possible, a basic rationale that (and this is the key phrase) *sorts out* those functions of government which should be primarily the responsibility of state and local governments and those which are appropriate for federal government leadership. This too was a central idea of the Nixon Administration's "New Federalism" program. Service functions of domestic government—such as education, employment and training, law enforcement, social services, community development—were regarded primarily as the responsibility of state and local governments. Federal aid in these fields, it was argued, should be in the form of revenue sharing and block grants to be administered at the discretion of state and local governments. Twenty billion dollars are estimated to be devoted to what the Office of Management and Budget calls "general-purpose and broad-based aid" in fiscal year 1980. If one excludes welfare grants from the analysis (as I believe we should), then this $20 billion accounts for 37 percent of total non-welfare federal grants-in-aid to state and local governments in 1980.[1]

On the other hand, the "New Federalism" policy, in *sorting out* functions, designated the group of programs which transfer income from the government to individuals (and there are quite a number of them) as programs which should be structured under equitable and uniform policies by the central government. These include programs such as social security, medicare, veterans' benefits, food stamps, and the supplemental security income program (SSI) passed in 1972 to aid the aged, blind, and disabled. All are programs that transfer income (either in cash or in-kind, as in the case of food stamps and medical care).

The reasons for centralizing policymaking for income-transfer programs was not only to make them equitable but to help ensure efficiency. In cases like

[1]This is a conservative estimate. If one classifies public service job funds allocated to state and local governments as "broad-based aid," then *one-half* of all federal grants for *other than* welfare purposes in 1980 would be in the form of "general-purpose and broad-based grants-in-aid." Office of Management and Budget, Special Analysis H, 1981 Federal Budget.

that of the social security system, the computer technology now available makes it possible to develop uniform records systems which assure that all citizens are treated the same and make it easier to root out duplication and fraud due to duplication.

THE ISSUE OF "WELFARE REFORM"

One major income-transfer program which is not as centralized as others is the cause of most of the clash and clang about "welfare reform." I refer to the program which aids families with children, headed by a parent or parents of working age. This group—adult parents and their children—was the target of Nixon's Family Assistance Plan, called FAP.[2] Although major reforms of income-transfer programs were made during the Nixon years (for example, the SSI program mentioned above was adopted), this part of Nixon's welfare program was not enacted.

Not to be outdone, President Carter grabbed this same nettle of transfer payments for poor families and their children and in 1977 advanced a plan much more sweeping and expensive than the Family Assistance Plan. Carter's new proposal was based on the "unanimous conclusion that the present welfare system should be scrapped and a totally new system implemented."[3] His ambitious $20 billion-plus proposal came in the form of a 163-page bill so intricate that few understood it and so controversial that fewer still (among experts and interested organizations) endorsed it. Carter's proposal, called the "Better Jobs and Income Program,"[4] met basically the same fate as FAP. It was criticized for going too far, expanding coverage too broadly, being too costly, and being grounded in theorizing that when looked at closely was fundamentally flawed. The basic question at this point became whether the nation should move (though slowly and carefully) toward the development of uniform and equitable policies applying to the transfer of income to the poor or if steps should be taken to overhaul the entire system all at once.

Many Republicans in the Congress took the position that Carter's Better Jobs and Income Program should be replaced by a more sensible plan that

[2]Richard Nixon proposed the Family Assistance Plan in a special message to the Congress, August 11, 1969. He call FAP "a new approach that will make it more attractive to work than to go on welfare, and that will establish a nationwide minimum payment to dependent families with children." FAP passed the House twice, but never the Senate.

[3]Jimmy Carter's press conference, May 2, 1977.

[4]Carter's Better Jobs and Income Program was unveiled August 6, 1977, almost eight years to the day after the announcement of FAP. (The plan was submitted to Congress, as H.R. 9030 and S. 2084, September 12, 1977.) It was put forth with much fanfare, though in this case the legislative response was tepid. Carter's plan, which was considerably more comprehensive than FAP, never came to a vote in the House and received little consideration in the Senate.

made changes in the existing program of aid to families with dependent children (AFDC)[5] on a step-by-step basis, that cost less, and which could be characterized as *incremental* rather than a radical restructuring approach.

THE REPUBLICAN INCREMENTAL REFORM APPROACH

On March 22, 1978, a Republican incremental bill (The Job Opportunities and Family Security Act, S. 2777) was introduced in the Senate by Senators Howard Baker (R-Tenn.), Henry Bellmon (R-Okla.), John Danforth (R-Mo.), Mark Hatfield (R-Ore.), Ted Stevens (R-Alaska), Milton Young (R-N.D.), and Abraham Ribicoff (D-Conn.). The sponsors were careful to point out that the bill's approach to welfare reform would improve the existing system rather than starting over from scratch. The bill was offered "not because it is a perfect answer to the welfare challenge," said Baker, "but because I think it is the best we can do at this time and marks a significant step forward in the process of trying to improve the welfare system."[6]

Danforth added:

> The welfare bill being introduced today does not attempt to turn the welfare system upside down. . . . We must be careful that any reforms we make do not just look good on paper but actually work. Therefore, our proposal does not throw away the old system, but makes critically needed and long called-for reforms in the context of that system.[7]

In the same vein, Bellmon stated: "The bill we introduce today starts with the assumption that we can and should build on the strengths and correct the weaknesses in current programs."[8] Key Republican Members of the House made similar statements in hearings though they did not introduce parallel legislation.[9]

This idea of an incremental approach to welfare policymaking had a far-reaching effect. On July 23, 1979, almost two years after submitting the Better

---

[5]The AFDC program originated as part of the Social Security Act of 1935 with the idea that it would aid widows and orphans during the Depression and "wither away" afterwards. It never did wither away. Estimated total spending (federal, state, and local) for AFDC in 1979 was $12.2 billion; estimated spending for its close cousin, the medicaid program established in 1965, was $20.3 billion in 1979, also including all levels of governmental expenditure (federal, state, and local). *Welfare Reform Background Papers: Data on Current Selected Programs, Report No. 79-83 EPW*, Congressional Research Service, Library of Congress, March 23, 1979.

[6]Congressional Record, March 22, 1978, p. S4308.

[7]*Ibid.*, p. S4309.

[8]*Ibid.*, p. S4310.

[9]Congressmen Al Ullman (D-Ore.) and James Corman (D-Calif.) introduced incremental welfare legislation, H.R. 4321, June 5, 1979.

Jobs and Income Program, the Carter Administration in a major turnaround conceded that this comprehensive plan was in trouble and introduced in its place an incremental welfare bill of its own, strikingly similar to the measure sponsored by Baker, Bellmon, et al.[10]

Then, as the old adage goes, a funny thing happened on the way to the forum. There emerged widespread support for *another* Republican alternative, an "alternative-to-the-alternative" in the form of block grants for the AFDC category. In effect, this approach says, take this piece of income-transfer policy, separate it out from the rest, and give it lock, stock, and barrel to the states to handle. This is the position Robert Carleson describes in this issue of *Commonsense*. I leave the particulars to him. There are larger questions of welfare policy that need to be treated here, questions about the proper role of different levels of government in American federalism.

"THE WELFARE MESS"

The U.S. income-transfer system is often portrayed as "a welfare mess," a term that is defined in a variety of ways. Some see the basic problem as fraud and abuse. Although it is true that problems remain, what needs to be emphasized is that as a result of efforts undertaken by Presidents Nixon and Ford, welfare error rates have been dramatically reduced in the past several years.[11]

Another common definition of the "welfare mess" is in terms of program proliferation—that there are too many intertwined and jumbled income-transfer programs. Some perspective is needed here. The welfare system, in short, consists of different strokes for different folks under income-transfer programs. There are "insurance-type" programs for unemployed and retired persons, supplemented by other programs for those too old or disabled to work who did not pay at all (or did not pay enough) into an insurance-type program. There are separate programs for veterans and for the working-age poor and their offspring. Certain needs are also identified separately for purposes of transferring income from the government to individuals. Health, housing, food, college education—all are needs which are treated separately under programs that transfer resources (either cash or in-kind) from the government to individuals based on need.

Is this really a mess? Maybe not. If we look at the history of income-trans-

---

[10]The Carter Administration's incremental welfare reform bill was submitted to the House of Representatives, July 23, 1979, as H.R. 4904.

[11]Welfare error rates were cut by more than half from 1973 to 1978. A July 11, 1979 Department of Health, Education, and Welfare statement compared error rates in AFDC which occurred in April–September 1973 and the same time period in 1978. In 1973, the percentage of dollar loss in overpayments and payments to ineligibles, was 16.5. In 1978, the error rate was 7.1 percent.

fer programs in other Western democracies, the picture is similar. These countries, too, have multiple programs with different strokes for different folks. And they have adopted them for the same reason we have, because the society views different conditions and needs differently.

NO TO GRAND SCHEMES FOR A GUARANTEED INCOME

I would argue that what the body politic wants to do should not be overridden by what some HEW intellectuals prefer in the way of simplistic and comprehensive reforms that would set up a single super system to replace all existing income-transfer programs with a new grand scheme for a guaranteed income.

However, the purpose of this article is not to argue against a new, fully-federalized program for a guaranteed income. Rather it is to urge that existing income-transfer policies should be integrated better. The history of the past 20 years (accelerated, in fact, from 1969 to 1977) has been in the direction of pulling these policies together. It makes sense to sort out functions so that this responsibility—making policies for income-transfer programs so they fit together better—should be the responsibility of the national government in American federalism. The values to be served are equity (treating all persons the same with allowances for regional differences in prices and wages) and efficiency. We are about to engage (one would hope so anyway) in a long overdue effort to reform health financing programs. This must be done with a careful eye to integrating such changes with other income-transfer programs.

ADMINISTRATIVE REFORM NEEDED

It is not enough to identify policymaking for income-transfer programs as a responsibility of the federal government. A critical point must be added: *Washington policymakers must do this job better.* Instead of rushing to the Hill quadrennially with a new grand scheme, policymakers in Washington must clearly and forthrightly take on the responsibility for improving the linkages among existing programs and the efficiency of the operations of the existing array of income-transfer programs. Much of this purpose could be achieved by regulatory and administrative action.

It is in this context that the incremental welfare reform bill pending in the U.S. Senate should be viewed. This bill, which passed the House in 1979, takes several steps to integrate programs and to treat family welfare recipients equitably.[12] This bill embodies the incremental approach of the March 1978 Senate

[12]S. 1290, which was introduced in the Senate, June 6, 1979, is pending in the Senate Finance Committee. H.R. 4904 passed the House of Representatives, November 7, 1979, by a vote of 222—184.

Republican bill and the similar Carter proposal (the second Carter welfare reform bill) submitted a year later. The House-passed bill would set a national minimum payment of 65 percent of the poverty level that would entail increased benefits in eight or possibly 10 states.[13] It would adopt new and now widely agreed upon standards for key aspects of eligibility. For example, a new flat-rate assets test applying to all cases in the same way would be adopted, whereas state laws now vary widely and, in some cases, involve detailed requirements that are very difficult to administer and often add to problems of program abuse and mismanagement. The House-passed bill would provide fiscal relief to state and local taxpayers by modestly increasing the federal share of payments under the AFDC program.[14] It would periodically revise the minimum payment under AFDC to keep up with the purchasing power of the dollar. It would provide aid to intact poor families with children as a way to prevent family breakup and hopefully prevent the further development of a culture of dependency among the nation's poor. It would integrate the food stamp and AFDC programs and in this way increase the capability of state and county administrative systems. In addition, the Republican incremental bill in the Senate would assign job priority for two-parent families, again as a way to help prevent the growth of welfare dependency.

The idea of a block grant for AFDC turns the clock back on welfare policy and would isolate the most controversial and vulnerable group of welfare recipients. It could result in competition by the states whereby some states would hold down benefits and tighten eligibility standards in ways that could eventually result in higher concentrations of the poor in the states with the most adequate welfare benefits. The fiscal strain on the receiving states versus their lower-benefit neighbors could cause imbalances in job and growth patterns. This is bad economics. The fact that people and jobs move in a free society is the underlying reason why the burden of financing welfare benefits should be shared on an equitable basis by the society as a whole.

An important distinction needs to be made here between policymaking and administration. The pending incremental reforms of the AFDC program move in the direction of more uniform national policymaking. They do not change the present state of affairs whereby the payments under the AFDC program are administered in some cases by states and in others by counties. Since it is the family headed by an employable person that needs services most—job

[13]The minimum would apply to AFDC benefits and food stamps combined.

[14]For AFDC and medicaid, the federal share ranged in 1977 from 50 percent in California, New York, and about 10 other states to 82.6 percent in Mississippi, 76.6 percent in South Carolina, and 74.6 percent inArkansas. The medicaid matching ratios are similar. For food stamps, only administrative costs are shared. The federal government pays the full amount of the benefits, and states and counties pay half of the administrative costs. *Welfare Reform Background Papers: Data on Current Selected Programs, op. cit.*

services, placement services, training, day care to aid working parents, etc.—it makes sense to have the payments to these families made by the governments which have the responsibility for these service-type programs.

In the process of sorting out governmental functions to assure accountability, the best long-run answer, I believe, is to have the policies for transfer payments made at the national level, with the federal government providing equalized grant-in-aid payments to state governments which administer some of these payments. The states under our constitutional system should design—each according to its own conditions and needs—a system for having social service programs (jobs, employment services, day care, foster care, institutions, and other services) administered in a way that is coordinated with the state-administered payment system for programs like AFDC and medicaid, which are partially financed under grants-in-aid from Washington.

SUMMING UP

To sum up, there are three basic directions for welfare policy: (1) grand scheme, super reforms to overhaul all welfare programs; (2) incremental rationalizing reforms; and (3) the block grant approach. It is always wise to stake out the middle ground. Still, it needs to be noted that both the grand scheme approach and the block grant approach are radical changes. And radical change always has its costs in terms of disruption and unanticipated consequences.

Some may not like this way of looking at the situation, but I see the incremental position—the middle ground—as the conservative position in terms of Burkean or institutional conservatism, building carefully and systematically on what we have in place.

Returning to the idea of a "welfare mess," I believe the "messiness" of our welfare policies is overrated. There have been improvements, as noted above, in reducing errors and abuses.

Recognizing that many values underlie the nation's various income-transfer programs, I argue that, with one exception, these programs are coming together in increasingly better ways—though there are needs for further changes. The one exception is health policy. It is not so much the "welfare mess" that we face as the "medicaid mess." That is where we should concentrate our energies now in terms of fundamental policy reforms.

When it comes to other income-transfer programs, the welfare policy debate has quieted down in recent years. An equilibrium of sorts has emerged. Traditional liberals don't assert in the same bold ways they used to that we need to adopt large increases in the amounts of income transferred. (By traditional liberals, I mean the kind that can get elected.) Conservatives, on the other hand, no longer express deep concern about the escalation of welfare rolls. Indeed, the escalation of welfare rolls is not occurring at anything like the rate it did in the late sixties and early seventies. The rolls in fact are going down.[15]

The present period is a time for rationalization and integration. It is not a time for radical change in income-transfer programs other than in the health area where the problems of equity, efficiency, and cost escalation are indeed severe. Looking at the big picture this way, I come down squarely against radical changes such as would be involved in the adoption of a block grant approach for AFDC to split off and devolve the policy responsibility for this most controversial and vulnerable group of income-transfer recipients.

Republicans should continue to urge the strengthening of state and local governments for those functions which aren't centralized and which should not be. This standard applies especially to service-type programs. Republican policymakers should at the same time urge the rationalization and systematization of income-transfer programs so that they are viewed together, increasingly as part of a system that treats all citizens the same, although in some cases with allowances for regional differences in prices and wages.

Document 8

Inaugural Address of President Ronald Reagan

Following the Swearing In as the 40th President of the United States. January 20, 1981

Senator Hatfield, Mr. Chief Justice, Mr. President, Vice President Bush, Vice President Mondale, Senator Baker, Speaker O'Neill, Reverend Moomaw, and my fellow citizens:

To a few of us here today this is a solemn and most momentous occasion. And, yet, in the history of our Nation it is a commonplace occurrence. The orderly transfer of authority as called for in the Constitution routinely takes place, as it has for almost two centuries, and few of us stop to think how unique we really are. In the eyes of many in the world, this every-4-year ceremony we accept as normal is nothing less than a miracle.

---

[15]Total recipients were 11.3 million in June 1975 (*Welfare Background Papers: Data on Current Selected Programs, op. cit.*) and 10.2 million in June 1979 (Staff Estimate, Princeton Urban and Regional Research Center, Princeton, New Jersey).

Mr. President, I want our fellow citizens to know how much you did to carry on this tradition. By your gracious cooperation in the transition process you have shown a watching world that we are a united people pledged to maintaining a political system which guarantees individual liberty to a greater degree than any other, and I thank you and your people for all your help in maintaining the continuity which is the bulwark of our Republic.

The business of our Nation goes forward. These United States are confronted with an economic affliction of great proportions. We suffer from the longest and one of the worst sustained inflations in our national history. It distorts our economic decisions, penalizes thrift, and crushes the struggling young and the fixed-income elderly alike. It threatens to shatter the lives of millions of our people.

Idle industries have cast workers into unemployment, human misery, and personal indignity. Those who do work are denied a fair return for their labor by a tax system which penalizes successful achievement and keeps us from maintaining full productivity.

But great as our tax burden is, it has not kept pace with public spending. For decades we have piled deficit upon deficit, mortgaging our future and our children's future for the temporary convenience of the present. To continue this long trend is to guarantee tremendous social, cultural, political, and economic upheavals.

You and I, as individuals, can, by borrowing, live beyond our means, but for only a limited period of time. Why, then, should we think that collectively, as a nation, we're not bound by that same limitation? We must act today in order to preserve tomorrow. And let there be no misunderstanding—we are going to begin to act, beginning today.

The economic ills we suffer have come upon us over several decades. They will not go away in days, weeks, or months, but they will go away. They will go away because we as Americans have the capacity now, as we've had in the past, to do whatever needs to be done to preserve this last and greatest bastion of freedom.

In this present crisis, government is not the solution to our problem; government is the problem. From time to time we've been tempted to believe that society has become too complex to be managed by self-rule, that government by an elite group is superior to government for, by, and of the people. Well, if no one among us is capable of governing himself, then who among us has the capacity to govern someone else? All of us together—in and out of government—must bear the burden. The solutions we seek must be equitable with no one group singled out to pay a higher price.

We hear much of special interest groups. Well, our concern must be for a special interest group that has been too long neglected. It knows no sectional boundaries or ethnic and racial divisions, and it crosses political party lines. It is made up of men and women who raise our food, patrol our streets, man our mines and factories, teach our children, keep our homes, and heal us when we're sick—professionals, industrialists, shopkeepers, clerks, cabbies, and truck drivers. They are, in short, "We the people," this breed called Americans.

Well, this administration's objective will be a healthy, vigorous, growing economy that provides equal opportunities for all Americans with no barriers born of bigotry or discrimination. Putting America back to work means putting all Americans back to work. Ending inflation means freeing all Americans from the terror of runaway living costs. All must share in the productive work of this "new beginning," and all must share in the bounty of a revived economy. With the idealism and fair play which are the core of our system and our strength, we can have a strong and prosperous America, at peace with itself and the world.

So, as we begin, let us take inventory. We are a nation that has a government—not the other way around. And this makes us special among the nations of the Earth. Our government has no power except that granted it by the people. It is time to check and reverse the growth of government which shows signs of having grown beyond the consent of the governed.

It is my intention to curb the size and influence of the Federal establishment and to demand recognition of the distinction between the powers granted to the Federal Government and those reserved to the States or to the people. All of us need to be reminded that the Federal Government did not create the States; the States created the Federal Government.

Now, so there will be no misunderstanding, it's not my intention to do away with government. It is rather to make it work—work with us, not over us; to stand by our side, not ride on our back. Government can and must provide opportunity, not smother it; foster productivity, not stifle it.

If we look to the answer as to why for so many years we achieved so much, prospered as no other people on Earth, it was because here in this land we unleashed the energy and individual genius of man to a greater extent than has ever been done before. Freedom and the dignity of the individual have been more available and assured here than in any other place on Earth. The price for this freedom at times has been high. But we have never been unwilling to pay that price.

It is no coincidence that our present troubles parallel and are proportionate to the intervention and intrusion in our lives that result from unnecessary and excessive growth of government. It is time for us to realize that we're too great a nation to limit ourselves to small dreams. We're not, as some would have us believe, doomed to an inevitable decline. I do not believe in a fate that will fall on us no matter what we do. I do believe in a fate that will fall on us if we do nothing. So, with all the creative energy at our command, let us begin an era of national renewal. Let us renew our determination, our courage, and our strength. And let us renew our faith and our hope.

We have every right to dream heroic dreams. Those who say that we're in a time when there are no heroes, they just don't know where to look. You can see heroes every day going in and out of factory gates. Others, a handful in number, produce enough food to feed all of us and then the world beyond. You meet heroes across a counter. And they're on both sides of that counter. There are entrepreneurs with faith in themselves and faith in an idea who create new jobs, new wealth and opportunity. They're individuals and families whose taxes support the government and whose voluntary gifts support church, charity, culture, art, and education. Their patriotism is quiet but deep. Their values sustain our national life.

Now, I have used the words "they" and "their" in speaking of these heroes. I could say "you" and "your," because I'm addressing the heroes of whom I speak—you, the citizens of this blessed land. Your dreams, your hopes, your goals are going to be the dreams, the hopes, and the goals of this administration, so help me God.

We shall reflect the compassion that is so much a part of your makeup. How can we love our country and not love our countrymen; and loving them, reach out a hand when they fall, heal them when they're sick, and provide opportunity to make them self-sufficient so they will be equal in fact and not just in theory?

Can we solve the problems confronting us? Well, the answer is an unequivocal and emphatic "yes." To paraphrase Winston Churchill, I did not take the oath I've just taken with the intention of presiding over the dissolution of the world's strongest economy.

In the days ahead I will propose removing the roadblocks that have slowed our economy and reduced productivity. Steps will be taken aimed at restoring the balance between the various levels of government. Progress may be slow, measured in inches and feet, not miles, but we will progress. It is time to reawaken this industrial giant, to get government back within its means, and to lighten our punitive tax burden. And these will be our first priorities, and on these principles there will be no compromise.

On the eve of our struggle for independence a man who might have been one of the greatest among the Founding Fathers, Dr. Joseph Warren, president of the Massachusetts Congress, said to his fellow Americans, "Our country is in danger but not to be despaired of. . . . On you depend the fortunes of America. You are to decide the important question upon which rests the happiness and the liberty of millions yet unborn. Act worthy of yourselves."

Well, I believe we, the Americans of today, are ready to act worthy of ourselves, ready to do what must be done to ensure happiness and liberty for ourselves, our children, and our children's children. And as we renew ourselves here in our own land, we will be seen as having greater strength throughout the world. We will again be the exemplar of freedom and a beacon of hope for those who do not now have freedom.

To those neighbors and allies who share our freedom, we will strengthen our historic ties and assure them of our support and firm commitment. We will match loyalty with loyalty. We will strive for mutually beneficial relations. We will not use our friendship to impose on their sovereignty, for our own sovereignty is not for sale.

As for the enemies of freedom, those who are potential adversaries, they will be reminded that peace is the highest aspiration of the American people. We will negotiate for it, sacrifice for it; we will not surrender for it now or ever.

Our forbearance should never be misunderstood. Our reluctance for conflict should not be misjudged as a failure of will. When action is required to preserve our national security, we will act. We will maintain sufficient strength to prevail if need be, knowing that if we do so we have the best chance of never having to use that strength.

Above all we must realize that no arsenal or no weapon in the arsenals of the world is so formidable as the will and moral courage of free men and women. It is a weapon our adversaries in today's world do not have. It is a weapon that we as Americans do have. Let that be understood by those who practice terrorism and prey upon their neighbors.

I'm told that tens of thousands of prayer meetings are being held on this day, and for that I'm deeply grateful. We are a nation under God, and I believe God intended for us to be free. It would be fitting and good, I think, if on each Inaugural Day in future years it should be declared a day of prayer.

This is the first time in our history that this ceremony has been held, as you've been told, on this West Front of the Capitol. Standing here, one faces a magnificent vista, opening up on this city's special beauty and history. At the end of this open mall are those shrines to the giants on whose shoulders we stand.

Directly in front of me, the monument to a monumental man, George Washington, father of our country. A man of humility who came to greatness reluctantly. He led America out of revolutionary victory into infant nationhood. Off to one side, the stately memorial to Thomas Jefferson. The Declaration of Independence flames with his eloquence. And then, beyond the Reflecting Pool, the dignified columns of the Lincoln Memorial. Whoever would understand in his heart the meaning of America will find it in the life of Abraham Lincoln.

Beyond those monuments to heroism is the Potomac River, and on the far shore the sloping hills of Arlington National Cemetery, with its row upon row of simple white markers bearing crosses or Stars of David. They add up to only a tiny fraction of the price that has been paid for our freedom.

Each one of those markers is a monument to the kind of hero I spoke of earlier. Their lives ended in places called Belleau Wood, The Argonne, Omaha Beach, Salerno, and halfway around the world on Guadalcanal, Tarawa, Pork Chop Hill, the Chosin Reservoir, and in a hundred rice paddies and jungles of a place called Vietnam.

Under one such marker lies a young man, Martin Treptow, who left his job in a small town barbershop in 1917 to go to France with the famed Rainbow Division. There, on the western front, he was killed trying to carry a message between battalions under heavy artillery fire.

We're told that on his body was found a diary. On the flyleaf under the heading, "My Pledge," he had written these words: "America must win this war. Therefore I will work, I will save, I will sacrifice, I will endure, I will fight cheerfully and do my utmost, as if the issue of the whole struggle depended on me alone."

The crisis we are facing today does not require of us the kind of sacrifice that Martin Treptow and so many thousands of others were called upon to make. It does require, however, our best effort and our willingness to believe in ourselves and to believe in our capacity to perform great deeds, to believe that together with God's help we can and will resolve the problems which now confront us.

And after all, why shouldn't we believe that? We are Americans.

God bless you, and thank you.

NOTE: The President spoke at 12 noon from a platform erected at the West Front of the Capitol. Immediately before the address, the oath of office was administered by Chief Justice Warren E. Burger.

The address was broadcast live on radio and television.

Document 9

The State of the Union

Address Delivered Before a Joint Session of the Congress. January 26, 1982

Mr. Speaker, Mr. President, distinguished Members of the Congress, honored guests, and fellow citizens:

Today marks my first State of the Union address to you, a constitutional duty as old as our Republic itself.

President Washington began this tradition in 1790 after reminding the Nation that the destiny of self-government and the "preservation of the sacred fire of liberty" is "finally staked on the experiment entrusted to the hands of the American people." For our friends in the press, who place a high premium on accuracy, let me say: I did not actually hear George Washington say that. [*Laughter*] But it is a matter of historic record. [*Laughter*]

But from this podium, Winston Churchill asked the free world to stand together against the onslaught of aggression. Franklin Delano Roosevelt spoke of a day of infamy and summoned a nation to arms. Douglas MacArthur made an unforgettable farewell to a country he loved and served so well. Dwight Eisenhower reminded us that peace was purchased only at the price of strength. And John F. Kennedy spoke of the burden and glory that is freedom.

When I visited this chamber last year as a newcomer to Washington, critical of past policies which I believed had failed, I proposed a new spirit of partnership between this Congress and this administration and between Washington and our State and local governments. In forging this new partnership for America, we could achieve the oldest hopes of our Republic—prosperity for our nation, peace for the world, and the blessings of individual liberty for our children and, someday, for all of humanity.

It's my duty to report to you tonight on the progress that we have made in our relations with other nations, on the foundation we've carefully laid for our economic recovery, and finally, on a bold and spirited initiative that I believe can change the face of American government and make it again the servant of the people.

Seldom have the stakes been higher for America. What we do and say here will make all the difference to autoworkers in Detroit, lumberjacks in the Northwest, steelworkers in Steubenville who are in the unemployment lines; to black teenagers in Newark and Chicago; to hard-pressed farmers and small businessmen; and to millions of everyday Americans who harbor the simple wish of a safe and financially secure future for their children. To understand the state of the Union, we must look not only at where we are and where we're going but where we've been. The situation at this time last year was truly ominous.

The last decade has seen a series of recessions. There was a recession in 1970, in 1974, and again in the spring of 1980. Each time, unemployment increased and inflation soon turned up again. We coined the word "stagflation" to describe this.

Government's response to these recessions was to pump up the money supply and increase spending. In the last 6 months of 1980, as an example, the money supply increased at the fastest rate in postwar history—13 percent. Inflation remained in double digits, and government spending increased at an annual rate of 17 percent. Interest rates reached a staggering 21½ percent. There were 8 million unemployed.

Late in 1981 we sank into the present recession, largely because continued high interest rates hurt the auto industry and construction. And there was a drop in productivity, and the already high unemployment increased.

This time, however, things are different. We have an economic program in place, completely different from the artificial quick-fixes of the past. It calls for a reduction of the rate of increase in government spending, and already that rate has been cut nearly in half. But reduced spending alone isn't enough. We've just implemented the first and smallest phase of a 3-year tax-rate reduction designed to stimulate the economy and create jobs. Already interest rates are down to 15¾ percent, but they must still go lower. Inflation is down from 12.4 percent to 8.9, and for the month of December it was running at an annualized rate of 5.2 percent. If we had not acted as we did, things would be far worse for all Americans than they are today. Inflation, taxes, and interest rates would all be higher.

A year ago, Americans' faith in their governmental process was steadily declining. Six out of 10 Americans were saying they were pessimistic about their future. A new kind of defeatism was heard. Some said our domestic problems were uncontrollable, that we had to learn to live with this seemingly endless cycle of high inflation and high unemployment.

There were also pessimistic predictions about the relationship between our administration and this Congress. It was said we could never work together. Well, those predictions were wrong. The record is clear, and I believe that history will remember this as an era of American renewal, remember this administration as an administration of change, and remember this Congress as a Congress of destiny.

Together, we not only cut the increase in government spending nearly in half, we brought about the largest tax reductions and the most sweeping changes in our tax structure since the beginning of this century. And because we indexed future taxes to the rate of inflation, we took away government's built-in profit on inflation and its hidden incentive to grow larger at the expense of American workers.

Together, after 50 years of taking power away from the hands of the people in their States and local communities, we have started returning power and resources to them.

Together, we have cut the growth of new Federal regulations nearly in half. In 1981 there were 23,000 fewer pages in the *Federal Register* which lists new regulations, than there were in 1980. By deregulating oil we've come closer to achieving energy independence and helped bring down the cost of gasoline and heating fuel.

Together, we have created an effective Federal strike force to combat waste and fraud in government. In just 6 months it has saved the taxpayers more than $2 billion, and it's only getting started.

Together we've begun to mobilize the private sector, not to duplicate wasteful and discredited government programs, but to bring thousands of Americans into a volunteer effort to help solve many of America's social problems.

Together we've begun to restore that margin of military safety that ensures peace. Our country's uniform is being worn once again with pride.

Together we have made a New Beginning, but we have only begun.

No one pretends that the way ahead will be easy. In my Inaugural Address last year, I warned that the "ills we suffer have come upon us over several decades. They will not go away in days, weeks, or months, but they will go away . . . because we as Americans have the capacity now, as we've had it in the past, to do whatever needs to be done to preserve this last and greatest bastion of freedom."

The economy will face difficult moments in the months ahead. But the program for economic recovery that is in place will pull the economy out of its slump and put us on the road to prosperity and stable growth by the latter half of this year. And that is why I can report to you tonight that in the near future the state of the Union and the economy will be better—much better—if we summon the strength to continue on the course that we've charted.

And so, the question: If the fundamentals are in place, what now? Well, two things. First, we must understand what's happening at the moment to the economy. Our current problems are not the product of the recovery program that's only just now getting underway, as some would have you believe; they are the inheritance of decades of tax and tax and spend and spend.

Second, because our economic problems are deeply rooted and will not respond to quick political fixes, we must stick to our carefully integrated plan for recovery. That plan is based on four commonsense fundamentals: continued reduction of the growth in Federal spending; preserving the individual and business tax reductions that will stimulate saving and investment; removing unnecessary Federal regulations to spark productivity; and maintaining a healthy dollar and a stable monetary policy, the latter a responsibility of the Federal Reserve System.

The only alternative being offered to this economic program is a return to the policies that gave us a trillion-dollar debt, runaway inflation, runaway interest rates and unemployment. The doubters would have us turn back the clock with tax increases that would offset the personal tax-rate reductions already passed by this Congress. Raise present taxes to cut future deficits, they tell us. Well, I don't believe we should buy that argument.

There are too many imponderables for anyone to predict deficits or surpluses several years ahead with any degree of accuracy. The budget in place, when I took office, had been projected as balanced. It turned out to have one of the biggest deficits in history. Another example of the imponderables that can make deficit projections highly questionable—a change of only one percentage point in unemployment can alter a deficit up or down by some $25 billion.

As it now stands, our forecast, which we're required by law to make, will show major deficits starting at less than a hundred billion dollars and declining, but still too high. More important, we're making progress with the three keys to reducing deficits: economic growth, lower interest rates, and spending control. The policies we have in place will reduce the deficit steadily, surely, and in time, completely.

Higher taxes would not mean lower deficits. If they did, how would we explain that tax revenues more than doubled just since 1976; yet in that same 6-year period we ran the largest series of deficits in our history. In 1980 tax revenues increased by $54 billion and in 1980 we had one of our all-time biggest deficits. Raising taxes won't balance the budget; it will encourage more government spending and less private investment. Raising taxes will slow economic growth, reduce production, and destroy future jobs, making it more difficult for those without jobs to find them and more likely that those who now have jobs could lose them. So, I will not ask you to try to balance the budget on the backs of the American taxpayers.

I will seek no tax increases this year, and I have no intention of retreating from our basic program of tax relief. I promise to bring the American people—to bring their tax rates down and to keep them down, to provide them incentives to rebuild our economy, to save, to invest in America's future. I will stand by my word. Tonight I'm urging the American people: Seize these new opportunities to produce, to save, to invest, and together we'll make this economy a mighty engine of freedom, hope, and prosperity again.

Now, the budget deficit this year will exceed our earlier expectations. The recession did that. It lowered revenues and increased costs. To some extent, we're also victims of our own success. We've brought inflation down faster than we thought we could, and in doing this, we've deprived government of those hidden revenues that occur when inflation pushes people into higher income tax brackets. And the continued high interest rates last year cost the government about $5 billion more than anticipated.

We must cut out more nonessential government spending and root out more waste, and we will continue our efforts to reduce the number of employees in the Federal work force by 75,000.

The budget plan I submit to you on February 8th will realize major savings by dismantling the Departments of Energy and Education and by eliminating ineffective subsidies for business. We'll continue to redirect our resources to our two highest budget priorities—a strong national defense to keep America free and at peace and a reliable safety net of social programs for those who have contributed and those who are in need.

Contrary to some of the wild charges you may have heard, this administration has not and will not turn its back on America's elderly or America's poor. Under the new budget, funding for social insurance programs will be more than double the amount spent only 6 years ago. But it would be foolish to pretend that these or any programs cannot be made more efficient and economical.

The entitlement programs that make up our safety net for the truly needy have worthy goals and many deserving recipients. We will protect them. But there's only one way to see to it that these programs really help those whom they were designed to help. And that is to bring their spiraling costs under control.

Today we face the absurd situation of a Federal budget with three-quarters of its expenditures routinely referred to as "uncontrollable." And a large part of this goes to entitlement programs.

Committee after committee of this Congress has heard witness after witness describe many of these programs as poorly administered and rife with waste and fraud. Virtually every American who shops in a local supermarket is aware of the daily abuses that take place in the food stamp program, which has grown by 16,000 percent in the last 15 years. Another example is Medicare and Medicaid—programs with worthy goals but whose costs have increased from 11.2 billion to almost 60 billion, more than 5 times as much, in just 10 years.

Waste and fraud are serious problems. Back in 1980, Federal investigators testified before one of your committees that "corruption has permeated virtually every area of the Medicare and Medicaid health care industry." One official said many of the people who are cheating the system were "very confident that nothing was going to happen to them." Well, something is going to happen. Not only the taxpayers are defrauded; the people with real dependency on these programs are deprived of what they need, because available resources are going not to the needy, but to the greedy.

The time has come to control the uncontrollable. In August we made a start. I signed a bill to reduce the growth of these programs by $44 billion over the next 3 years while at the same time preserving essential services for the truly needy. Shortly you will receive from me a message on further reforms we intend to install—some new, but others long recommended by your own congressional committees. I ask you to help make these savings for the American taxpayer.

The savings we propose in entitlement programs will total some $63 billion over 4 years and will, without affecting social security, go a long way toward bringing Federal spending under control.

But don't be fooled by those who proclaim that spending cuts will deprive the elderly, the needy, and the helpless. The Federal Government will still sub-sidize 95 million meals every day. That's one out of seven of all the meals served in America. Head Start, senior nutrition programs, and child welfare programs will not be cut from the levels we proposed last year. More than one-half billion dollars has been proposed for minority business assistance. And re-search at the National Institute of Health will be increased by over $100 mil-lion. While meeting all these needs, we intend to plug unwarranted tax loopholes and strengthen the law which requires all large corporations to pay a minimum tax.

I am confident the economic program we've put into operation will pro-tect the needy while it triggers a recovery that will benefit all Americans. It will stimulate the economy, result in increased savings and provide capital for ex-pansion, mortgages for home building, and jobs for the unemployed.

Now that the essentials of that program are in place, our next major un-dertaking must be a program—just as bold, just as innovative—to make gov-ernment again accountable to the people, to make our system of federalism work again.

Our citizens feel they've lost control of even the most basic decisions made about the essential services of government, such as schools, welfare, roads, and even garbage collection. And they're right. A maze of interlocking jurisdic-tions and levels of government confronts average citizens in trying to solve even the simplest of problems. They don't know where to turn for answers, who to hold accountable, who to praise, who to blame, who to vote for or against. The main reason for this is the overpowering growth of Federal grants-in-aid pro-grams during the past few decades.

In 1960 the Federal Government had 132 categorical grant programs, cost-ing $7 billion. When I took office, there were approximately 500, costing nearly a hundred billion dollars—13 programs for energy, 36 for pollution control, 66 for social services, 90 for education. And here in the Congress, it takes at least 166 committees just to try to keep track of them.

You know and I know that neither the President nor the Congress can properly oversee this jungle of grants-in-aid; indeed, the growth of these grants has led to the distortion in the vital functions of government. As one Demo-cratic Governor put it recently: The National Government should be worrying about "arms control, not potholes."

The growth in these Federal programs has—in the words of one intergov-ernmental commission—made the Federal Government "more pervasive, more intrusive, more unmanageable, more ineffective and costly, and above all, more [un]accountable." Let's solve this problem with a single, bold stroke: the return of some $47 billion in Federal programs to State and local government, together with the means to finance them and a transition period of nearly 10 years to avoid unnecessary disruption.

I will shortly send this Congress a message describing this program. I want to emphasize, however, that its full details will have been worked out only after close consultation with congressional, State, and local officials.

Starting in fiscal 1984, the Federal Government will assume full responsibility for the cost of the rapidly growing Medicaid program to go along with its existing responsibility for Medicare. As part of a financially equal swap, the States will simultaneously take full responsibility for Aid to Families with Dependent Children and food stamps. This will make welfare less costly and more responsive to genuine need, because it'll be designed and administered closer to the grassroots and the people it serves.

In 1984 the Federal Government will apply the full proceeds from certain excise taxes to a grassroots trust fund that will belong in fair shares to the 50 States. The total amount flowing into this fund will be $28 billion a year. Over the next 4 years the States can use this money in either of two ways. If they want to continue receiving Federal grants in such areas as transportation, education, and social services, they can use their trust fund money to pay for the grants. Or to the extent they choose to forgo the Federal grant programs, they can use their trust fund money on their own for those or other purposes. There will be a mandatory pass-through of part of these funds to local governments.

By 1988 the States will be in complete control of over 40 Federal grant programs. The trust fund will start to phase out, eventually to disappear, and the excise taxes will be turned over to the States. They can then preserve, lower, or raise taxes on their own and fund and manage these programs as they see fit.

In a single stroke we will be accomplishing a realignment that will end cumbersome administration and spiraling costs at the Federal level while we ensure these programs will be more responsive to both the people they're meant to help and the people who pay for them.

Hand in hand with this program to strengthen the discretion and flexibility of State and local governments, we're proposing legislation for an experimental effort to improve and develop our depressed urban areas in the 1980's and '90's. This legislation will permit States and localities to apply to the Federal Government for designation as urban enterprise zones. A broad range of special economic incentives in the zones will help attract new business, new jobs, new opportunity to America's inner cities and rural towns. Some will say our mission is to save free enterprise. Well, I say we must free enterprise so that together we can save America.

Some will also say our States and local communities are not up to the challenge of a new and creative partnership. Well, that might have been true 20 years ago before reforms like reapportionment and the Voting Rights Act, the 10-year extension of which I strongly support. It's no longer true today. This administration has faith in State and local governments and the constitutional balance envisioned by the Founding Fathers. We also believe in the integrity, decency, and sound, good sense of grassroots Americans.

Our faith in the American people is reflected in another major endeavor.

Our Private Sector Initiatives Task Force is seeking out successful community models of school, church, business, union, foundation, and civic programs that help community needs. Such groups are almost invariably far more efficient than government in running social programs.

We're not asking them to replace discarded and often discredited government programs dollar for dollar, service for service. We just want to help them perform the good works they choose and help others to profit by their example. Three hundred and eighty-five thousand corporations and private organizations are already working on social programs ranging from drug rehabilitation to job training, and thousands more Americans have written us asking how they can help. The volunteer spirit is still alive and well in America.

Our nation's long journey towards civil rights for all our citizens—once a source of discord, now a source of pride—must continue with no backsliding or slowing down. We must and shall see that those basic laws that guarantee equal rights are preserved and, when necessary, strengthened.

Our concern for equal rights for women is firm and unshakable. We launched a new Task Force on Legal Equity for Women and a Fifty-States Project that will examine State laws for discriminatory language. And for the first time in our history, a woman sits on the highest court in the land.

So, too, the problem of crime—one as real and deadly serious as any in America today. It demands that we seek transformation of our legal system, which overly protects the rights of criminals while it leaves society and the innocent victims of crime without justice.

We look forward to the enactment of a responsible Clean Air Act to increase jobs while continuing to improve the quality of our air. We're encouraged by the bipartisan initiative of the House and are hopeful of further progress as the Senate continues its deliberations.

So far, I've concentrated largely, now, on domestic matters. To view the state of the Union in perspective, we must not ignore the rest of the world. There isn't time tonight for a lengthy treatment of social—or foreign policy, I should say, a subject I intend to address in detail in the near future. A few words, however, are in order on the progress we've made over the past year, reestablishing respect for our nation around the globe and some of the challenges and goals that we will approach in the year ahead.

At Ottawa and Cancún, I met with leaders of the major industrial powers and developing nations. Now, some of those I met with were a little surprised that I didn't apologize for America's wealth. Instead, I spoke of the strength of the free marketplace system and how that system could help them realize their aspirations for economic development and political freedom. I believe lasting friendships were made, and the foundation was laid for future cooperation.

In the vital region of the Caribbean Basin, we're developing a program of aid, trade, and investment incentives to promote self-sustaining growth and a better, more secure life for our neighbors to the south. Toward those who would export terrorism and subversion in the Caribbean and elsewhere, especially Cuba and Libya, we will act with firmness.

Our foreign policy is a policy of strength, fairness, and balance. By restoring America's military credibility, by pursuing peace at the negotiating table wherever both sides are willing to sit down in good faith, and by regaining the respect of America's allies and adversaries alike, we have strengthened our country's position as a force for peace and progress in the world.

When action is called for, we're taking it. Our sanctions against the military dictatorship that has attempted to crush human rights in Poland—and against the Soviet regime behind that military dictatorship—clearly demonstrated to the world that America will not conduct "business as usual" with the forces of oppression. If the events in Poland continue to deteriorate, further measures will follow.

Now, let me also note that private American groups have taken the lead in making January 30th a day of solidarity with the people in Poland. So, too, the European Parliament has called for March 21st to be an international day of support for Afghanistan. Well, I urge all peace-loving peoples to join together on those days, to raise their voices, to speak and pray for freedom.

Meanwhile, we're working for reduction of arms and military activities, as I announced in my address to the nation last November 18th. We have proposed to the Soviet Union a far-reaching agenda for mutual reduction of military forces and have already initiated negotiations with them in Geneva on intermediate-range nuclear forces. In those talks it is essential that we negotiate from a position of strength. There must be a real incentive for the Soviets to take these talks seriously. This requires that we rebuild our defenses.

In the last decade, while we sought the moderation of Soviet power through a process of restraint and accommodation, the Soviets engaged in an unrelenting buildup of their military forces. The protection of our national security has required that we undertake a substantial program to enhance our military forces.

We have not neglected to strengthen our traditional alliances in Europe and Asia, or to develop key relationships with our partners in the Middle East and other countries. Building a more peaceful world requires a sound strategy and the national resolve to back it up. When radical forces threaten our friends, when economic misfortune creates conditions of instability, when strategically vital parts of the world fall under the shadow of Soviet power, our response can make the difference between peaceful change or disorder and violence. That's why we've laid such stress not only on our own defense but on our vital foreign assistance program. Your recent passage of the Foreign Assistance Act sent a signal to the world that America will not shrink from making the investments necessary for both peace and security. Our foreign policy must be rooted in realism, not naivete or self-delusion.

A recognition of what the Soviet empire is about is the starting point.

Winston Churchill, in negotiating with the Soviets, observed that they respect only strength and resolve in their dealings with other nations. That's why we've moved to reconstruct our national defenses. We intend to keep the peace. We will also keep our freedom.

We have made pledges of a new frankness in our public statements and worldwide broadcasts. In the face of a climate of falsehood and misinformation, we've promised the world a season of truth—the truth of our great civilized ideas: individual liberty, representative government, the rule of law under God. We've never needed walls or minefields or barbed wire to keep our people in. Nor do we declare martial law to keep our people from voting for the kind of government they want.

Yes, we have our problems; yes, we're in a time of recession. And it's true, there's no quick fix, as I said, to instantly end the tragic pain of unemployment. But we will end it. The process has already begun, and we'll see its effect as the year goes on.

We speak with pride and admiration of that little band of Americans who overcame insuperable odds to set this Nation on course 200 years ago. But our glory didn't end with them. Americans ever since have emulated their deeds.

We don't have to turn to our history books for heroes. They're all around us. One who sits among you here tonight epitomized that heroism at the end of the longest imprisonment ever inflicted on men of our Armed Forces. Who will ever forget that night when we waited for television to bring us the scene of that first plane landing at Clark Field in the Philippines, bringing our POW's home? The plane door opened and Jeremiah Denton came slowly down the ramp. He caught sight of our flag, saluted it, said, "God bless America," and then thanked us for bringing him home.

Just 2 weeks ago, in the midst of a terrible tragedy on the Potomac, we saw again the spirit of American heorism at its finest—the heorism of dedicated rescue workers saving crash victims from icy waters. And we saw the heroism of one of our young government employees, Lenny Skutnik, who, when he saw a woman lose her grip on the helicopter line, dived into the water and dragged her to safety.

And then there are countless, quiet, everyday heroes of American life—parents who sacrifice long and hard so their children will know a better life than they've known; church and civil volunteers who help to feed, clothe, nurse, and teach the needy; millions who've made our nation and our nation's destiny so very special—unsung heroes who may not have realized their own dreams themselves but then who reinvest those dreams in their children. Don't let anyone tell you that America's best days are behind her, that the American spirit has been vanquished. We've seen it triumph too often in our lives to stop believing in it now.

A hundred and twenty years ago, the greatest of all our Presidents delivered his second State of the Union message in this chamber. "We cannot escape

history,'' Abraham Lincoln warned. ''We of this Congress and this administration will be remembered in spite of ourselves.'' The ''trial through which we
pass will light us down, in honor or dishonor, to the latest generation.''

Well, that President and that Congress did not fail the American people.
Together they weathered the storm and preserved the Union. Let it be said of
us that we, too, did not fail; that we, too, worked together to bring America
through difficult times. Let us so conduct ourselves that two centuries from
now, another Congress and another President, meeting in this chamber as we
are meeting, will speak of us with pride, saying that we met the test and preserved for them in their day the sacred flame of liberty—this last, best hope of
man on Earth.

God bless you, and thank you.

INDEX